HEADDOWNPUSHING

What Is Your Message?

Marques C. Roberts

Copyright © 2018 by Marques C. Roberts

All rights reserved.

ISBN **978-0578422602**

Dedication

From as far back as I can remember you've been my teacher. You directly taught me sports, video games, dances, music, and fashion when we were young and as we grew you indirectly taught me individuality, competitiveness, toughness, fearlessness, boldness, humility, passion, and hard work. When it was my turn to lead the program in High School I realized you showed me how to set myself apart, how to pursue my dreams, how to not accept the status quo, how to be unapologetically me, how to lead, how to believe in myself, and how to walk my own path. As we became young men you protected me even when I didn't want protection, you held me accountable when I didn't hold myself accountable, you challenged me when I failed to challenge myself, and you loved me when I didn't want to be loved. As men you cheered me on, you celebrated me, and you even honored/humbled me by telling me that you looked up to me.

The truth is I'll forever be looking up to you and I'll be forever grateful to do so. When I thought I was beyond following my big brother you tended to do something new or different that made me kick things up a notch. Even in leaving me you gave me something I'll spend the rest of my life working towards and I'll need every second of that time to even come close to being the person you are.

As I sit here writing this dedication I can't believe this is my new reality. Today is exactly three weeks to the day that you left us. While I'm still hurting and saddened by your passing I'm more honored and grateful for the time we had because I can't imagine what my life would be like without you. Thank you Big Bruh for everything! For putting the ball in my hands, being my first role-model, setting the bar, setting the tone, for loving our parents, loving our family, loving me unconditionally, loving my wife, loving my kids, loving our elders, loving life, loving the grind, and possessing a selfless love for people.

People will be talking about your Home Going Celebration for years to come. Hundreds to thousands came forth to honor you because the special being you are made that big of an impact. We hurt, we cried, we laughed, we consoled, we encouraged, we celebrated, and we're forging on differently because of you. I tried my damnedest to do you proud…hope you approved. That was not the end though Pooh it was merely the beginning. Thank you for doing you and being unapologetically Pooh because that is the difference. You doing what you believed in, you not compromising, you making your own way on your terms has left a mark on the world that will live on through others for generations to come.

When I began writing this book I knew the message I wanted to get across, I just was not sure of how I would do so. That being said, I didn't seek approval, I just did what you've always told me to do…I did me. The thing is though, throughout the entire time of my writing I had no clue you were living the book. I thought about you on many occasions as I wrote and how I wanted you to have a copy. Now I sit here realizing you were helping me write and had been doing so all my life. Your life is validation for everything I've written. Pooh, with everything in me, I just want you to know I love you; I dedicate this book to you as you truly had your HeadDownPushing and your message continues to speak loudly in your physical absence.

Love & Miss you dearly,

Lil Bruh

Preface

Growing up, like most children, I admired the presence of people who commanded respect. The presence, charisma, notoriety, money, regard, love, and possessions were all appealing, but for me, more than anything, it was the respect I admired. Respect for the person, not the persona, always stood out to me because it crossed the lines of race, class, religion, age, and sex. Whether it was the Insurance Man, greeter at the local H.E.B., the teacher who went the extra mile, Pastors, town officials, drug dealers, cafeteria cashier, school secretary, or the many other individuals who commanded or carried themselves with respect; I remember being enamored with how they carried themselves and how others responded to them because it truly struck me how these things were not the same for everyone.

I also noticed the difference early on from my front row seat to my parent's lives as I observed a certain level of respect that others reserved for them. What stood out the most to me was the difference in the walks of life of the people who displayed this respect— Young knuckleheads in and out of trouble, wives of city officials, respected drug dealers, police chiefs, pastors, doctors, party girls, teachers, the elderly, and drug addicts. Something key that I didn't realize early on was that their respect for my parents was a reciprocation of the respect my parents gave. No matter the race, class, religion, past, or current circumstances, they treated everyone as a person of value. More importantly, they conducted themselves as people of value and never let how you treated them or anyone else make them disrespect themselves by acting out of character. This taught me that respect should not have to be earned; it should be given as a reflection of the level of respect I have for myself…Because If I treat you like you treat me, that makes me just like you.

My mother and father modeled the moral compass and work ethic that set the framework of the foundation of the person I should be in a me-first culture. They allowed me to make my own decisions regarding where my life was headed, which I am forever grateful for, because the pain of the mistakes I made play a huge role in my decision-making today. The bumps and bruises forced me to learn to trust myself and that more trust is built through my investment. In identifying how my parents were treated, I was able to see how others were treated differently by the same people, how others perceived these people, and most importantly, how others allowed themselves to function in a space that displayed a lack of respect for themselves. Witnessing these interactions and studying people pushed me to want to carry that element of respect forward for my family's name; I thought I would assume this naturally, but I would first have to learn to see my value as God's creation with no attachments (social status, athletic ability, possessions, or awards). Then I had to learn to live those values in order to build enough respect for myself to understand if I have to go outside my values it's not worth it. When I say it's not worth it, I am not referring to the result I am referring to the compromise. This is the compromise of our self-respect and self-trust that leads so many of us spiraling out-of-control because of the letdown, the inconsistency, the loss of trust, the loss of respect, and the loss of faith.

Do you know your value, or do you use what you possess to determine how you feel about yourself? Has compromising your values hurt or diminished your self-respect and/or self-trust? What do you allow in your life from yourself and others that you know you're better than? What in your life do you want to change, but don't trust yourself to change it? No one is coming to save you from you. You have to learn who you are in God's eyes then hold yourself accountable to do the work to rebuild your trust and respect for yourself so God can use your message to teach others to do the same.

Table of Contents

HEADDOWNPUSHING I

DEDICATION III

PREFACE V

CHAPTER 1: HEADDOWNPUSHING 1

CHAPTER 2: FAITH 16

CHAPTER 3: HUMILITY 32

CHAPTER 4: FOCUS 57

CHAPTER 5: COURAGE 82

CHAPTER 6: WILLINGNESS 101

CHAPTER 7: CONSISTENCY 119

CHAPTER 8: ACCOUNTABILITY 147

CHAPTER 9: PATIENCE 163

CONCLUSION 180

ACKNOWLEDGEMENTS 201

Chapter 1

HeadDownPushing

Life has a way of delivering blows that hit us so hard spiritually, mentally, and/or physically that we close our minds off to the endless opportunity that life offers when we seek to make our way. Life also has a way of discreetly chipping away at our sense of self-worth through cultural norms and influential people in our lives by creating a cycle of accepting, suppressing, and conforming until we identify as inferior; ultimately relieving ourselves of determination, ambition, and hope. In response to our experiences, instead of making our way, we choose the comfort of settling in the lies and excuses of our circumstances as our truth to avoid the pain or discomfort we encounter when chasing our dreams or living in expectation. It's imperative that we learn to understand the pain of life's punches in those specific moments is temporary. So when the pain or hurt leaves we have to learn to leave that space too and get back to living. Or else we end up wasting days, weeks, months, even years stuck existing in that place of hurt and pain because we don't realize we're held captive by what we're trying to avoid.

While some of us run others simply give up. The sad part is many of the people who give up only see the loss they've endured and never consider the victory that accompanied the loss. Every individual must endure something when they choose to make a way in life. The turbulence and challenges of life can catch us off guard and lead to circumstances where the life we desire and the person we have the potential to become exist as written off ideals we subconsciously determine to be unattainable. That life and that person are treated like unrealistic fantasies in our minds, so we never act on them, allowing something that lives in us to become dormant or even die. With the death of the dream/vision, we also lose our innocent ambition, freedom of thought, pureness of heart, and limitless curiosity that allow us to live life with an authenticity and boldness that fulfills our spirit and breathes life into others.

Everyone gets discouraged and even quits for periods of time, but no one should ever totally give up on themselves because life has beaten them down. Disbelief, discouragement, loss of faith, misery, discontent, sadness, pain, pain, and more pain should be expected as a part of becoming or pursuing more, not avoided. As we grow in knowledge and maturity, the process changes what we perceive as painful and how we deal with that pain. I didn't say we stop facing hard times or that we stop being hurt, but we learn to allow our pain to teach us to learn from our experiences in order to deploy what we learned when we encounter new challenges, in new places, through new people, with new forms of attack.

Growing through the process enables us to be more confident in decision-making and builds a new perspective that changes the impact hard times have on our mentality. We all possess what it takes to consistently face the challenges associated with overcoming ourselves, but few are willing to submit to the work. You won't stop learning of yourself if you submit and your perspective will change if you let go of your pride, but reaching this place requires having faith to believe in something that you don't know exists within you.

Some of what you are reading may be pushing you to question yourself, which is a good thing because you will become more aware of your own circumstances and how you function in them. You or someone you know is being challenged with facing themselves and taking ownership of the work to be done in the midst of "perceived" unfavorable circumstances. This is one of the toughest steps of progression, taking ownership of your role in your misfortune and addressing how you get out of your own way, because regardless of what influenced your decision, you stopped you. Whether you are the employee who questions his/her ability to sit at the head of the table in the boardroom due to the stereotypes you have witnessed your entire life, the young man who refuses to step up because he cannot see past what he believes he lacks, the kid who is uncomfortable with the life he and his friends are leading but refuses to pursue what is on his heart because he does not know what that looks like, the young lady who is tired of the routine but does not know it is okay to go without or go in spite of as she endures the process of progression, the person who loses a piece of themselves daily as they conform to the culture of the workplace instead of facing the unknown on the other side of quitting their job, the restless individuals frustrated with the emptiness of prioritizing status instead of investing in substance to provide themselves peace, or the countless people who feel stuck as they have settled in the face of standards they accepted that suggest they are inadequate, it does not matter, because the process of moving forward begins with taking ownership of your circumstances.

One of the toughest periods of my life began in college and continued for about 8 to 10 years after college as I transitioned from being a student, to being in the workforce, to intentionally building myself and my career. From Jr. High through college, the day to day structure of school/athletics, the requirements to be academically eligible to participate in sports, and graduate provided direction, gave me a sense of purpose, and helped establish goals for Marques, the football player (athlete), to work towards achieving. Once I finished school and football was no longer an option the structure school and sports provided my life for the past 18 years could no longer mask, my lack of self-worth, lack of direction, and my sense of purpose as a person. Like most young men and women in those same circumstances, as recent graduates with no plan, I had no clue what I was experiencing, I didn't know what to do, and I didn't know the only true obstacle in my way was me. The reality that life is waiting on you to dictate what happens, not your circumstances, is not something every individual realizes at the same time and no two people have the same reaction when faced with the challenges of transitioning into dictating your path versus following the path set before you.

When I left college I was walking away with a college degree & a successful college football career, but I didn't have a clue about where my life was headed nor did I have a clue about how to respond to what life was about to ask of me. I was banking on accolades, relationships, and opportunity to just make things fall into place; totally dismissing the value of the investment I had made over the past 20+ years that garnered the accolades and brought me to this position. With time I would learn the true value was not in what the work produced in degrees and awards, the true value was in the work revealing what I had in me and what the work built in me. Whether you have to or choose to drop out in Jr. High, have a career ending injury, quit college/technical school or retire as a professional athlete; every individual has that moment where life asks for more from the person that you are. When and how you hear life asking has nothing to do with your title, class, status, accomplishments, finances, talent, race, sex, religion, or any other social standard we use to measure ourselves and others. Life's questions and your answers have everything to do with your core values, self-awareness, self-worth, and faith.

It took structure leaving my life for me to realize I had no control. I relied so heavily on sports that I had minimal self-awareness away from the game so it wasn't until the game was gone and I was drowning in my misery that I realized my sense of my self-worth was gone. Without the game I could no longer avoid, mask, or ignore my pain. Not knowing what I was dealing with and not being willing to explore my emotions led me to a point where I was compromising my core values daily. Then one day fatigue and discomfort with my unfulfilling lifestyle brought me to a place where I only had my faith and my faith told me it was time to take ownership of my life away from this person I allowed circumstances to create. Faith introduced me to purpose which introduced me to my self-worth. My self-worth pushed me to look at my life and the value of my effort in the lives of others encouraged me to be more aware of who I am and my tendency to not own that piece of me. With a renewed sense of self through faith I gained vision and vision provided my new structure. This does not mean that my old ways of thinking and bad habits went away, I got my life plans all figured out, and I now have a positive attitude daily that makes every day great. This means when life asks for more from me I know I am capable so I don't allow me to get in my own way. It means when I say no to something my no's have to be substantial, not excuses, because when I settle I'm tormented as refusing to give more feels too similar to relinquishing control. My renewed sense of self also means that when self-awareness told me to look back I saw that my trials weren't meant to defeat me, they were meant to complete me. And what they built in me only prepared me for the trials ahead. Now, knowing who I am and believing in the man I am, my days are no longer spent running from life's challenges, instead I spend my time submitting to what my vision is requiring of me to make my way.

You Change Your Life When You Change How You Think

As youth, information and experience are stamped on our brains as we retain our experiences and most of the information we consume. Through time some of us begin to realize the way things should be or could be is admirable and exciting, but it's the way things are that actually shapes our being and our perspective. Most people don't even understand this is happening; they go their entire lives never realizing they have been living according to what they could not see in themselves, and what they would not see in others. The cultural norms we live by make it very easy to fail to acknowledge the impact of our surroundings because external influence is a constant and internal limitations are constantly reinforced by the world we are confined to. Whether it's race, age, sex, class, social status, self-esteem, perspective, etc. we hurt ourselves and others by what is embedded because it's the only thing we know. Empathy enables us to step out of our bubble into someone else's experience in order to gain understanding. In 2018 most people wish others had more empathy because of all the division being created through political posturing and the hidden agendas of various groups in our society. The thing is we first need to look at ourselves and consider the impact of the culture we know that teaches us that one's life experience is due solely to their actions or the culture that teaches us to conform because we can't see ourselves beyond what we know.

As much as I wanted to turn away from a mentality and behaviors that I knew would stifle me as a person, living in a world that constantly reinforced that way of thinking became a part of me despite my intent and effort to strive for better. Knowing that the world tried to rob me of my willingness to take my life where I wanted, I am eternally grateful for my parents and their commitment to cultivating a sentiment of "more" in my life. From exposing me to more outside of the community, pushing me past settling to asking more of myself, directing my attention to those who required more from themselves, protecting me from my own ignorance of the demand of more in character, showing me what giving more looks like, allowing me to feel the consequences of less, teaching me I should expect more from myself, and telling me that more is required from you when you are blessed with more. I cannot place a value on what they instilled me, but I can say the seed they cultivated grew into something within that saved my life when the world was having its way with me.

As an African American youth in my community of Luling Texas, our culture did not empower us as individuals. Please understand this is not a knock on the community I love as I could sense people cared for me everywhere I went regardless of their color. I'm simply speaking to cultural norms we experienced on a day to day basis in regards to our education and norms within the community. We weren't taught, through what we witnessed, to study physicians or lawyers like we were taught to praise and glorify athletes and dope boys (drug dealers). No owner of a major business, no city or law enforcement official, or no person in educational leadership was black. There was no one in the leadership roles around town that we learned about in school whose life represented the sentiment of *"It is up to me to be more if I want more for myself."* My dad would even shake my hand on the regular so I could feel the roughness & callouses on his hands then he'd tell me "Make sure to get your education so you can get you a good job, so your hands won't end up like this". He was pushing me in the right direction, but he didn't realize what he was living was more empowering as he had started his own business through sheer will, quality, integrity, and consistency. I don't hold what we missed out on against anyone because everyone was operating based on what they knew; I just know what I didn't see made me close off mentally to seeing certain opportunities as a possibility.

A difference maker in my self-worth (along with my parent's being intentional about exposure) was the love from various people in the community. As an athlete it was normal to be praised and placed on a pedestal, especially as young black men. So being encouraged as a young man away from sports was vital because that love and positivity was transferred to the person I was and the person I was becoming…I had received their message. Being treated with respect and feeling cared for meant a lot because it made you feel valued by someone other than family. Several people even made it their personal duty to encourage us about our future after High School. This made a difference in our lives as well because it suggested they saw more than what many of us reduced ourselves to. There are an innumerable amount of gestures that my friends and I could rattle off, but the truth is when you see yourself as inferior you have to learn that is not your truth. If not, you'll always operate based on that lie and nothing anyone does or says can save you from you.

Even though every sentiment of positivity sent my way, from numerous sources, meant the world to me; what we lived, in regards to seeing ourselves as secondary or inferior, validated the exact opposite of those positive sentiments. In response to seeing/experiencing things as they were, I approached all activities away from sports like I was at a deficit because I saw myself as inadequate. I was told I was smart, but at the same time I was constantly reminded to talk this way or other fashion was superior. I equated what came naturally to me as lesser-than and I felt like many of my personal preferences were inappropriate; convincing me that if the majority of my being was inappropriate, from my sense of style, my choice of music, to how I spoke, etc. then I'm operating at a disadvantage because I have to learn to not be myself in order to be successful. These thoughts and feelings made me seek external approval for self-approval. I had subconsciously accepted the lie that I was inferior, so I strived for accomplishment, awards, and notoriety to create a feeling of value in myself. This would suffice for snippets of time, but this false sense of self-worth would end as soon as life would ask something of Marques the person. It was evident that while I was confident in my gifts and/or talent as an athlete, I was not confident in me away from sports.

In small towns in Texas, the norm for many young men and women is to graduate from high school and immediately seek a modest job that you believe you are worthy or capable of. Most don't pursue higher education or an alternate career route because it is easier to accept mediocrity when you are oblivious to the need to or refuse to convince yourself you are capable of more. Most students, like those before them, feel people like them aren't corporate leaders or don't own their own businesses because of the limits they accepted as "the way things are." A lot of us, regardless of race, gender or class, were told lies about what we could or couldn't accomplish and more lies about the "only" way to be successful by people who spoke from a place of pure ignorance. While what these people said was impactful, the damage was already done because those lies were embedded in our day-to-day existence. Still to this day many individuals are uninformed of their options and for many others they're disinterested because they're convinced they're incapable.

Accepting the standards created by society as a measuring stick of my worth made me question all that I was and validate all that I was not. Even though I had the will to work, instead of expecting success, I would sell myself short in anticipation of doors closing or things falling through. I recall being conflicted growing up because people encouraged me with words, but their actions suggested they did not truly mean what they were saying. I did not understand that this was a reflection of what that person could conceive as possible, not a reflection of what I was capable of so instead of dismissing many of them I allowed their limits to become my truth.

I envisioned myself flourishing in corporate America at times, but the world suggested, and I believed, sports were my ticket to do something that truly mattered. If football didn't work out I felt I was supposed to aim for what I could physically see or what felt practical, but I should not waste my energy on pursuing a professional career, as that would be virtually impossible and somewhat foolish. So years later when I found myself in those exact circumstances where football was no longer an option, my biggest obstacle became finding a way to believe I could be successful away from sports. The power of the internal struggle to believe in yourself is so powerful that people literally opt out of life. You can find men and women of all races, ages, classes, and religions who suffer from depression, alcoholism, and many other issues stemming from the fact that they continue to choose not to believe enough in themselves to face the challenges/obstacles of pursuing the life they desire. On top of the many routine distractions we adopt to ease the pain or enable us to ignore our emotions, we begin championing and celebrating the lifestyle of accepting less from ourselves.

I vividly remember an ongoing joke with my friends about not wanting to go out of our comfort zone because we feared embarrassment and the unknown associated with new experiences. We envisioned, misinterpreted, and discussed opposition from others looking down on us or not wanting us to succeed so often that it became a reality in our minds when we had no evidence to support these theories. In all actuality we had people in our corner who wanted us to succeed. They were just waiting on us to put forth the effort and make ourselves available to be helped. The part that hurts me is bullying played a major role in why I conformed to this mentality. As I think through this period of my life I get upset about what I allowed people to do to me and what I did to myself to appease them. Like most targets of bullies, people took their insecurities out on me. In response I dimmed my light to avoid bringing attention to myself. As time passed on their insecurity became more evident and as my closest friends and I grew up we began to grow away. The thing I admire the most about growing away is we never talked about why we stopped hanging around with everyone; we just did our own thing.

Not stepping out of our comfort zone was funny for a period of time, but the same way we separated from the negativity, we should have separated from the complacent mentality. While there was opposition, obstacles, and bias towards us the truth is everything we claimed that was in our way was an excuse that we created and/or embraced to avoid facing the fact that we were unwilling to submit to what our vision was asking of us. Looking back, it stings to know we missed out on countless opportunities for exposure and eye-opening experiences because of fear, pride, immaturity, and complacency.

In college, I noticed similar jokes amongst my teammates evolved from fear and lack of confidence to external projections of insecurity and bitterness. I witnessed my friends stereotype and call other people names because they didn't subscribe to the closed-minded mentality that was hurting us. This is when I began to realize my silence in those moments felt familiar to the silence I felt before straying away from the huddles in Luling when other people became the topic of conversation. The uneasiness I felt this time around pushed me to learn more about what I was missing out on because even though sports and social status made others accept me I never let go of my outsider mentality I developed growing up. I walked away from the huddles when I was accepted, because I remembered people in those huddles attacking me. Being bullied made me feel like I never wanted to make someone feel lesser than because of the pain it caused me. Being immature and weak I laughed at the jokes at times, but I would have long conversations with the guys/gals who were picked on about how they picked up certain interests or how long they had been involved in certain groups or hobbies. The norms of the hows and the whys of those conversations always stuck with me because I recognized the power in the limits and bias they did not acknowledge and the significance of their boldness for what they were passionate about.

That willingness to do what you like when it is unpopular and boldly investing in what makes you happy is life changing because the experience of exploration teaches you discomfort comes before progress. They may have heard many jokes thrown their way, but the work they were doing on themselves was serious business. A couple years down the road when I realized I had no career path to fall back on outside of football I had to face the truth that the joke was now on me as I failed to explore and challenge myself in other areas of life away from sports that would add to me as a person. This aspect of my life left such a bad taste in my mouth that now, as an adult, I speak up if I witness someone exhibiting closed-mindedness. I refuse to accept it, embody it, or promote it, because it is not the mentality I want to project onto my children or anyone around me.

I catch myself if I feel the urge to puff my chest out with pride and say, "That ain't for me" simply because it's new or against the norm. I have learned to let the outsider have rule now embodying that willingness and boldness to explore to learn more about the world and myself.

One example of closed-mindedness that comes to mind is food. My wife and I like to try food from different cultures. When she talks about Indian or Vietnamese dishes, some friends and family members shake their heads and say, "I don't eat that; that stuff will make you sick," even though they've never eaten the food. Some even go as far to say, "Black people don't eat that," jokingly, but seriously. It is not abnormal for us to have to challenge the source of the thought process and the negativity associated with it to convince them to explore. Only to end up eating meals that they can't believe they enjoyed and making it a point to let it be known that they plan to come back with or without us.

When we embrace falsities to conform to the culture around us, we serve as the saboteur for ourselves and those closest to us. We say the perfect things to stroke our ego then avoid doing anything outside of our comfort zone to protect our pride. As time passes we witness our children do the same thing with the same foolish pride. This is the total opposite of what we should be doing to build the lives we desire as this only leads to living comfortable lives where we say a lot and do nothing to add to the person that we are becoming. Instead, we should speak minimally but do a lot in order to refresh our being and update our perspective.

It is vital for your progression that you examine where you have conformed and why because once you identify it, you can undo those emotions, thoughts, and behaviors going forward. Undoing the routine emotions, thoughts, and behaviors has changed my life which is why I wrote this book; to aid you in pulling back the veil on the lies you have accepted as truths; the same lies you have been avoiding that prevent you from believing in you. I'm not trying to sell you a gimmick to get rich quick; I'm selling you, you so you can do the work to establish a new internal foundation to support you realizing God's vision for your life.

What Is Your Message?

HeadDownPushing is embracing eight principles faith, focus, courage, accountability, willingness, consistency, patience, and humility to reinforce a lifestyle of seeking and fulfilling God's will in every opportunity despite your circumstances, influencing others to do the same. God's will is hidden in our experiences, so it is up to us to push aside self-serving agendas, selfish preferences, and prideful hesitance to seek God's will to be the message he intended to deliver to and through our lives. The ongoing process of seeking and fulfilling God's will in every opportunity is "being the message" and how do you be the message? You keep your HeadDownPushing.

How we approach, endure, respond, react, laugh, and cry along our journey of life delivers a message to those that we love, tolerate, befriend, mentor, encounter, and those just watching. Every interaction, verbal and non-verbal, has the power to impact a life. People often disregard waving, saying hello, holding doors open, smiling at someone, and giving compliments to strangers as common, routine, or insignificant, but this mentality does not acknowledge our value or significance as individuals. Accept that you are a significant vessel and take ownership of the power of your message by remaining mentally present even in what may seem like the most insignificant moments.

HeadDownPushing changes from person to person and applies differently for every individual to everyday situations in all walks of life. Athletes, greeters, models, entertainers, bloggers, teachers, actors, siblings, eating habits, marriage/relationships, on the job, relationship with Christ, career advancement, parenting, education, fighting disease, exercising, aunts/uncles, guardians, divorce, etc. are all examples of roles or instances where we should have our HeadDownPushing. In being the message, the message we send and receive is invaluable. I read a quote that said, "Kind words can be short and easy to speak, but their echoes are truly endless." I have found this statement to be true, as words of others from as far back as my childhood echo in my mind today. I also believe that the best of us lives on in the rest of us. Those things we live from the soul and share in the lives of others connect us as the aura, the passion, the love, the purity, the innocence, the joy and the freedom is passed on from person to person, from generation to generation. We place a target on the back of teachers, police officers, and Pastors assuming these roles imply you are willing to be held responsible for the guidance and insurance of others. But, we fail to realize that every individual has a target on their back as a servant, influencer, mentor, teacher, protector, etc. with varying responsibilities to different degrees.

The direct power of our actions is tremendous, but the indirect power is just as if not more influential. For instance, when you pay for someone's meal/drink in the drive-thru. You relieve that individual of the burden of paying for their purchase, but in doing so you may inspire that person to pay for the car behind them which triggers a chain reaction. Sometimes the same thing happens in the grocery line where an individual pays for the items of the person behind them in line and through seeing or hearing someone cover someone else's tab others are inspired to do the same. Understanding this, I know my responsibility is greater than what has been depicted throughout my life, in this book. My responsibility includes stepping out of my comfort zone to write this book and faithfully sharing this book with the world. Whether the book is received by 1 or 100 million, the execution enables me to be the message that God intends for not only everyone who reads the book or discusses the book, but also those who will have an interpretation of my writing the book.

The principles of HeadDownPushing help push you to a place where you find yourself doing things you would never have considered. Notice I said help and push, then let that sink in, because embracing the principles is not easy and they're not some sort of guaranteed plan for a perfect life. Like anything new you've attempted in the past, you will fall short. Embracing the principles means tough times are to be expected, but you allow your experiences, through living the principles, to diminish those old internal limits while leading you through the adversity of external obstacles and internal defeat. Accepting these experiences as your truth allows you to redefine yourself and challenge yourself to give more to life instead of simply desiring more from life. Once we get out of our own way to consistently give more to life, we initiate the process of shifting from dreaming to living the life we desire as God uses us and our actions to implore others to do the same.

What is your message? What is your life saying? What is your life not saying? Are you ready to get out of your own way and take ownership of your message? Your life's message creates hope, activates change, inspires dreams, destroys doubt and does the exact opposite as well. Yes, your life, the way you live not what you say, hope for, or point to alters the course of the lives of others. So it's time you take ownership of being the message you want to see in the lives of others.

For a period of time I was a lost young man with an assumed direction who did not like his life or who he had become. I eventually tapped into a hunger to do more with my life after learning my fears were based on lies because my life was created with purpose. In the following chapters, I share the eight principles of HeadDownPushing that I learned to embrace. We explore how changing my perspective pushed me to reinterpret my truth about prior experiences by looking into my past, seeking God's will in my experiences, and seeing how His will played a larger role than I ever could have imagined. We also look into how fighting to keep your HeadDownPushing reinforces your significance through purpose. With each principle I detail how relationship, not religion, reinforces God's love and will for our lives and reinforces our responsibility as His vessels in the lives of those who have been entrusted to us.

As you read, analyze the impact the principles have had or have not had on your life thus far. Peer into my personal stories to experience lessons from my journey to help you identify your own personal experiences you could've misinterpreted or simply refused to grow through. As you identify how the principles have been applied, were absent, or were overlooked in your life you will discover how your perception of past experiences can redefine your present and expand your expectations of your future.

Chapter 2

FAITH

The Unwavering Continuation on the Path God Has Determined for Your Life Without Knowing What Lies Ahead

For years, the power and truth of faith have been minimized and, at times, lost in the practice of religion. This has led to generations of people who stayed or strayed away from God because of how Christianity and other religions used their standards to drive others away instead of being inspired by relationship to pull them closer. Jesus scolded those who used religion and laws to edify themselves, but despite His stance, the same teachings have continued for centuries. Religious people, who lack relationship, remove God's grace and mercy, and replace it with standards to push others down instead of loving them up as Christ did. The mindless following of routines and rules don't bring us closer to God. Praying, reading the Bible, and continuing on the path God has created for our lives to bring Him glory are pillars of a life that not only inform us of His will, but also encourage and lead us to seek His presence as they add to our relationship with Him. The greater the relationship, the more we seek to be in His will. The further down the path faith takes us, the greater the challenges we encounter, but how we handle the challenges change as we come to understand that where we end, God picks up. This knowledge infuses us with a determination that doesn't allow us to peacefully go back to being the same person who routinely disregards His will. With our former routine becoming less desirable, we begin to lead our lives in the opposite direction with less resistance because the conclusion of the unconscious routine is all too familiar. Instead, we become more aware of our time and responsibility, enabling faith to guide us to where God wants us to be instead of settling or being complacent.

Through faith, we find ourselves volunteering our time where we used to avoid lending of ourselves and we hear ourselves speaking up in moments we used to be quiet; we experience a shift as we find ourselves seizing more and more opportunities that we previously thought we would never encounter. New business ventures, higher education, speaking up despite intimidation, philanthropy, filling out job applications, ignoring the unknown, facing the odds…this is faith personified, this is HeadDownPushing.

The first layer of faith is believing in God. The second layer of faith is believing in the gospel of Jesus Christ for salvation. The third layer of faith is what faith looks like. Personally, I would love for everyone to believe in the gospel, but I understand that is not necessary to have an all-conquering faith, nor do we have to believe in the gospel to have purpose. The dilemma for a person who is of tradition and not of relationship is that they become so consumed with the standard of how a believer should look and operate that they forget faith looks different through each vessel, as we all have individual personal assignments. The true personification of faith is Jesus, and our lives should be modeled after His. We should be metaphors of faith, in the lanes that we have been assigned, not studying others to condemn them for falling short, pretending to be something we are not capable of, or competing for selfish desires God did not intend for us.

Despite having different paths to travel Earvin "Magic" Johnson and Peyton Manning both became successful athletes and businessmen. Growing up, Magic Johnson's father worked as many as three jobs at a time, and Peyton Manning's father played in the NFL. So while Magic and Peyton may occupy similar positions of influence today, both painted their own picture of faith as they continued down the path God determined for their lives.

Peyton had to manage the pressure of great expectation and growing up in the shadow of the highly regarded Phenom, Archie Manning. This required a great measure of faith from Peyton as every mistake or misstep is magnified and weaponized to attack your being when you are the child of a public figure. Magic, on the other hand, had a completely different experience. What Peyton experienced as a norm as the son of a professional athlete, Magic's parents had to make it a point to expose him to. They had to be intentional about exposing him to all that life had to offer and teaching him the hard work it would take to create the life he desired. Imagine the level of faith he had to embody as a teenager to go against the norms of what he knew to pursuit something he had not seen (Hebrews 11:1 'Now faith is the substance of things hoped for, the evidence of things not seen'). While learning he had to set his sights on something greater than what he saw in his community, Magic also learned the values of hard work by working with his father as a garbage man. As he worked he faced ridicule from his peers who mocked him for working as a garbage man. If that wasn't enough he was even more faithful as he was bussed across town to a school where he wasn't welcomed and boldly chose to face racism head-on just to play the game he loved.

Magic and Peyton were a different race, class, and age in different states with different beginnings, different life experiences that created different perspective, as they faced different hurdles—whether it was accusations of sexual assault as a college athlete for Peyton Manning that led the questioning of his character or being forced to retire after contracting the HIV virus as the face of the NBA for Magic Johnson.

Despite whatever challenges they encountered along the way, they owned their lane. They may have lost a few battles in their lifetime, but they both have shown numerous people the faith it takes to get the upper-hand in the war against yourself. In embodying the faith it took to keep being the best version of themselves, they have impacted millions of lives as they changed culture in their respected sport and our country. They are what faith looks like.

This list goes on and on where you have individuals with similar lives in the present, but their journey and their ongoing message connects to and empowers people far beyond their imagination from the same side and polar opposite sides of the spectrum with similar impact. From Beyoncé and Madonna, Cardi B. and Taylor Swift, Michael Jordan and Larry Bird, Mookie Betts and Mike Trout, Lena Waithe and Quentin Tarantino, to Howard Stern and Charlamagne Tha God. LeBron James, who is his own entity, even took it upon himself to validate the power of our message, by giving tribute to Will Smith & Dave Chappelle because of the impact they had on his life through watching them bring greatness to their crafts. LeBron's statement speaks to the power we possess through our message. Chappelle and Smith weren't playing basketball when they inspired LeBron Still their approach and commitment to excellence inspired a young inner-city kid to demand excellence from himself as he embarked on his own journey.

There are countless ways people try to measure the impact of athletes or celebrities, which at times discredits the true value they add to humanity. The influence these men and women have on the perspective of people from different races, classes, sexes, age groups, and religions by simply bringing the best of themselves to their platforms is immeasurable. In acknowledging the magnitude of their impact, what we cannot afford to do is limit the responsibility of life-changing impact to famous people and discredit our own ability to influence others. When we place these limits on ourselves, we deny ourselves the experience of the power in being the message and fail to pass it on to someone else all because we refuse to faithfully lead our lives as we were called to do so.

We all fall short of God's standard, by action or circumstance, but that does not make us more or less of a believer. It is what we do despite falling short that displays our faith. Seeking to do His will after falling short implies great faith, which is necessary to continue when life consistently suggests you should quit or you won't be successful. Your path may be similar, but never identical, to any other life that came before you, so use their actions/experiences as information for your journey, not roadblocks that limit your faith. You were not brought to your circumstances to learn how to survive, you were brought there to show others how to live. It is time to let go of living within the confines of what you have learned and change your environment by being faithful enough to live in pursuit of what your heart desires.

The Power of Purpose

The definition of purpose is the reason for which something is created or exists. If you pay close attention to this definition then you automatically see two validations of purpose in your life, creation and existence. In my opinion knowing we are created with specific intent and we are still here for a reason makes purpose one of the greatest gifts we possess. Take a moment to let the power of the truth that there is specific reason for your being to sink in. Knowing you are God's vessel created with specific characteristics, on a specific path, to complete specific assignments, with a specific intent is invaluable. Discovering the sentiment of purpose and being faithful that you have a purpose charges us with redirecting our lives by validating the value and significance of our existence. This is critical because when we fail to own the sentiment of purpose in our lives we live like it.

Take a moment to consider why you allow or allowed yourself to live with no sense of direction. The truth is we don't value ourselves or our time because we lack knowledge of and we lack relationship with the source of our beliefs. We know terminology and routines/religious practices by heart, but we've failed to invest in learning of God or your source of faith through experience. Therefore most of us spend our time aimlessly going through life reacting to what happens to us when we should be waking up each day attacking life with specific intent.

There is something reaffirming about believing you were created for a reason. Instead of questioning yourself, you begin to move based on the answers God has already provided (In the Bible or your source of truth). This means when you go about your days you think and behave based on assignment and being equipped for assignment instead of external influences/personal preferences derived from fear, selfishness, pride, or ego that led to you settling into lifeless routines. This does not mean you don't have bad days, you don't have days where you don't feel like doing anything, or days where you're not as productive as you would like because you will. The difference is you just won't be able to be at peace when you have these type of days because you hold yourself accountable to make each day count to fulfill your assignment as you are humbled by God's love and reminded God's purpose for your life is bigger than you.

My mother and my great-aunt have always stressed the importance of knowing God through praying and giving time to God, but I never truly understood what knowing or fully experiencing Him meant until I felt like I had nothing else to give and He stepped in. Up until these few experiences at Baylor University, I would say I honored Him, but I only knew of Him. I can remember being alone in my apartment staring at the walls telling myself no one cared if I was alive and hating the fact that my life was not going the way I wanted (deeply engulfed in my pity-party). Because of where I wasn't I saw myself as a lost cause. This is a direct indication that I lacked a sense of purpose, because I discredited everything that I was based on what I felt I wasn't achieving without even considering how God sees me or His specific intent in my experiences. When I would finally reach a place where I was tired of being bitter, angry, depressed, and cold I would conclude my pity-party. Then I'd begin to pray more, read the Bible more, and find any way I could to spend more time with God until I felt like my burdens had been relieved. This didn't include any type of fixed routine, just a process of me getting to a point where I was able to completely submit myself to Him as I released whatever I was holding on to.

The good thing was that I knew something was not right with me; the bad thing was I was too heavily influenced by the world around me to understand the source of my feelings and the truth of what was happening in me as I spent more time with Him. Each time I had these internal bouts, after my pity party, I would shift my focus from selfish to selfless, i.e., from anger, self-pity, girls, partying, and notoriety to God, family, joy, love, and hard work. Like clockwork, things changed—I would be less angry, restless, and depressed, but I failed to realize not being consistent with where I dedicated my time was only a fix, not a solution. I continued this routine of only seeking Him in helpless moments through college and into the workplace until I became exhausted with the empty cycle of up and downs and desired more peace and substance in my life.

This time period was an emotional roller coaster for me because I lacked fulfilment. Not knowing purpose pushed me to turn to external influences around me for guidance, which led me to seek validation to fill a void that only purpose can fill. If I felt the people I wanted to see me saw me in the light I wanted I was good, but if that reassurance was not there in the capacity I needed it then there was no way to know how I might feel or behave. The irony is even though I was operating in selfishness when I did choose to put my best foot forth I made an impact on the world around me, but sadly I was completely oblivious to the impact because my self-centeredness would not allow me to see past me and the fickle standards I was chasing. This is a very important point because aimlessness or lack of purpose not only makes us miss out on being fulfilled, but also makes us discredit our value by making us overlook our impact and that we're being used by Him.

Owning purpose and knowing God incentivizes a new perspective. A perspective where purpose reminds us to do the opposite of allowing tasks and settings to define us and/or determine our value by placing our focus on His will and all that He has for us to discover in each experience as His vessel.

As you think of your existence, it is vital that you understand your specific experiences are a part of who you are becoming. They shape you spiritually, mentally, and physically to bring only what you can bring to the universe as God's vessel. This encourages me to keep my HeadDownPushing because of the significance we have in shaping the world and the impact doing so has on our family, friends, coworkers, teammates, spectators, associates, enemies, or anyone our lives impact directly or indirectly.

What you were born into, what you suffered through, and what you thought defined you are all behind you. It is up to you to release the negativity you are holding on to and embrace the power within gained from those experiences. It is God's will that we are humbled in our journey so we can identify how we have grown through life's ups and downs. Humility also reveals that no matter how bad things seem, if we are willing vessels, God uses our experiences to bring glory to Himself. With more understanding of purpose I realized that even though my journey hasn't aligned with the hopes and dreams of my youth, it helped mold and shape me. This discovery reshaped how I see myself, how I see others, and how I see the world around me as I understood it's our responsibility to accept each occurrence not as a part of our burden, but as a part of our significance to serve God's purpose.

The Power of Relationship

Every individual must come to a point where they realize they are responsible for their own relationship with God. Mama's or grandma's prayers cannot build or sustain the relationship God seeks to have with you. Many of us are introduced to religion at an early age where we are taught prayers, meditation, traditional rituals in and out of Church, and various forms of customary worship. In these teachings, we are taught how to be religious and why our faith is important. The issue with these teachings is, because so much emphasis is placed on how to be religious, the value of why is lost. We don't know why we pray, why we worship, why we read the Bible, or why we are Christians. This focus on how, for many people, led to a tradition of empty routines that lack the mindfulness and a spiritual hunger to experience the presence of God.

We often hear the statement, "I'm trying to find myself." We allow this statement to undermine God's truth because we fail to understand what it means to have a relationship with Christ. Who could possibly be a better source of information than He that predestined your life? We are not supposed to struggle to find ourselves and then look to God. We need to turn to Him so He can show us who we truly are in order to learn how to navigate our struggles.

Being lost is to be out of touch with God, and to be present with Him is to be at peace. Notice I said at peace, not found. On this journey, if we are willing, we continuously become who He predestined us to be so "finding you" is ongoing. Peace is a portion of what makes relationship so important. Life is up and down, so things may be better or worse at times regarding finances, family, job status, and life plans, but being in His presence makes the difference in how we deal with these times. It reminds us He has been and He will be present with us. That's peace, being able to deal with the ups downs and surprises of life while not losing sight of all that we have to be grateful for. His peace in our life calms us in the midst of chaos, steadies us in the face of opposition, and enlightens us by relieving us of the distractions we hold onto.

The power of relationships is often overlooked, but long before titles are given or roles are assigned, we are transformed by relationships. Whether it was a boyfriend/girlfriend, manager/coworker, teacher/mentor, or becoming a parent/guardian, most of us have experienced love for or from an outside source that moved us so greatly that it brought about an evolution in our being. This newly found selfless servant comes face to face with the selfish slave that creates conflict with every decision we make. The evolution in your being is apparent as you become more considerate, thoughtful, and open-minded because you are no longer the priority or the central focus in your decision- making. You get up earlier, you go to bed later, you eat what others prefer, you choose to dedicate your personal time to a specific service, you consider the well-being of others or the greater good of what has been entrusted to you over your own interests, you begin to seek what you can give, knowing that in your giving, you are receiving.

In the same manner, we experience the evolution of our being through relationships with people; we experience greater evolution through our relationship with Christ. This relationship is where we learn that our lives are a journey, an everlasting process of becoming all that God desires for us to be. As we faithfully forge on relationship reassures that our path in life is not happened upon, so through every experience, our desire to see God's will in our circumstances increases. We prioritize identifying what God is doing in us and through us so that we can be reassured we are on the path he predestined for us because of the disarray, frustration, and restlessness we experienced when we were headed in the wrong direction. The same way a bond with teammates or friends creates an experience within experiences is exactly what God desires to share with us through relationship.

To understand God's will for your life, you must make a commitment to seeing all circumstances through a Godly filter. Be with Him daily on your Journey, faithfully stepping out of the identity you have accepted for who He created you to be to step up and submit yourself to the process inviting God to show up in your circumstances as only God can. Going into every situation with God's will as the driving force and ultimate goal is how we invest in relationship and pull our destiny to us. Faith builds relationship, and through relationship our faith is increased if we allow. Faith says go and relationship says I got you. Even when the outcome is not what we want relationship reminds us if we keep faithing it the experience will do us more good than harm in the long run.

Prioritize your relationship so His influence can change your life. Allow faith, the foundation of HeadDownPushing, to fuel your relationship as you experience the presence of God in your life daily because without faith, we have no relationship.

In the book of Samuel, David the shepherd boy decided to accept the challenge of a Philistine super soldier, Goliath, based on His faith. He was confident in his ability and unwavering in His approach because He knew something about himself the others did not.

In David's days as a shepherd, he had won battles against bears and lions. Through these adverse situations, David saw that he had abilities he was previously unaware of, so he stayed faithful to what he had witnessed of himself and what he witnessed of God in his life.

World-renowned author Malcolm Gladwell says that researchers have uncovered that men, like David, who used a sling during this period were accurate enough to knock birds out of the sky and hit their targets with an impact equivalent to that of a .45 caliber handgun from distances of up to 200 yards. You and I know it takes a tremendous investment to develop a skill, and that is no ordinary skill. The process of spending day after day performing the same action, seeing your ability progress from novice, to intermediate, to advanced, to elite, is a huge investment. This process instills confidence and faith in your ability because, as you progress, you are witnessing the return on your investment firsthand. David experienced this each day as a shepherd protecting his flock, hunting, and practicing with the sling; therefore, faith would not allow him to turn away from the challenge of Goliath. He was a firsthand witness of his own ability. So in the moment of truth, it was necessary that David act based on what God had revealed to Him about himself and not succumb to a losing perspective or pressure to fight this fight in the manner that the others suggested. As many of us know, that is exactly what young David did by volunteering for the challenge the other men would not, going to battle without the standard armor, and questionably taking his nonthreatening sling as His weapon of choice to slay the giant beast Goliath.

We live in a world full of giants in the form of standards, stereotypes, prototypes, bias, prejudice, and many other facets of limits that coerce us to be close-minded regarding our own abilities and possibilities for our lives. Your journey has brought you to places where God "picked up" as well. You have overcome struggles with lions and bears of this world in which you gained strength and knowledge that you did not have before. It is time to be faithful to what you witnessed of yourself in those struggles; it is time to invest in who those experiences created and slay the giants standing before you. Like David, trust in what God has revealed to you and step out in faith knowing you can succeed, you will get the job done, and be humbled that while you may not be typical, that does not mean you are not capable.

What You Think Causes You to Miss Opportunities; How You Think Causes You to Miss Out on Life

This quote speaks to a moment-to-moment or day-to-day perspective, which is a reflection of an overall way of thinking. Because we fail to give new things a chance or see challenges as blessings/opportunities, we miss out on seeing our lives and the lives of others changed by our message in these moments. The experience of being vulnerable or uninformed but forging on in faith changes us by forcing us to focus on God's will, not the circumstances. It takes a great deal of faith to not second guess yourself or not be apprehensive in unchartered waters, but we only rob ourselves of experiencing our fullest potential when we turn away from the unknown or allow fear to make us play it safe.

When I signed my scholarship to play football at Baylor University, my only goal was to be the same person I was in high school and show everyone I was capable of being the leader they needed. That is a pretty steep goal for an 18-year-old, no-name recruit from Luling, Texas, population 4,661. But I knew if I was faithful to who God created me to be, I could get it done. Within the first week, instead of stepping up as the leader I set out to be, I became a spectator. I always observe and become familiar with my surroundings before acting, but in this case, I shifted from observing to assimilating. By choosing not to lead, I unconsciously chose to follow. I conformed to the culture that suggests freshmen are unqualified and should take a back seat, follow upperclassmen, and not say or do anything to make others feel uncomfortable about "the way things are."

When my class arrived in Waco, TX for two-a-days in the fall of 2000, there was not a winning culture in place, new leaders needed to step up and change the environment, but I could not see it in myself because my perspective minimized who God saw me as and maximized how I saw myself. After a good start in football that first semester, I spiraled out of control for the next two years. Letting circumstances dictate my life led me to follow others and seek distractions in the form of drugs, alcohol, and women to drown out the noise in me created by not being faithful enough to be a leader.

During my sophomore season, our head coach was fired and a new regime took over the football program. Not long after they arrived, they held a meeting for everyone who had a GPA below 2.0 in the proceeding semester — I was one of them. As I sat in our meeting room listening to the coaches tell us, "You have one semester to get your shit together." I asked myself, "How did you let yourself get here?" I had always been in honors or advanced classes since 4th grade. I had a couple of slippages as a teenager, but I never felt my life was out of my hands. I looked around the room at my teammates and decided that day to retake control of my situation. I decided I had to separate myself from the habits and the people who were pulling me away from where I wanted to be as a person (leader) and as a player (NFL). I saw a shift in my life as I hung out with different people and ventured outside the norm to occupy my time. I was able to seize more opportunities at different events because my perspective had changed. I supported fellow teammates engaged in activities outside of football, I engaged in student events like water balloon fights, I coached my teammate's Intramural basketball team, and I even went to a few events to see other students display their talents like music and oratorical skills. I was available and enjoying, not wallowing in depression, but I continued to miss out on life as I was still not bold enough to step into the role that was waiting for me.

The next season was better, but still nothing to write home about. The fear of the unknown, of how stepping up would be received, and not knowing if I truly was capable of being a leader was stronger than my faith. By the time the season ended, I was so frustrated with myself that I decided the person I had become had no more room in my life. The fire inside me held captive by fear, low self-esteem, and the unknown had become unbearable. I decided to no longer let anything stop me from doing what I felt was right in my heart. When offseason started in January, I went from the back of the line to leading drills and challenging my teammates to do the same. Every day I did what felt natural; I worked as hard as I could when others would just go through the motions. I went to the stadium early and watched film when the season was months away. Not long afterward, I noticed I was smiling from the inside, and for the first time at Baylor, I felt free to be unapologetically me. I did not have time to wonder what anyone thought, because I was constantly focused on moving in the right direction and I did not care if I ruffled anyone's feathers because I knew my heart was in the right place. The freedom that faith provides is the result of being settled in the spirit or being awakened by the peace the life you ran from provides.

We all have heard the saying "Fake it until you make it," but life has taught me to "Faith it until you awaken it." Faith leads us and pushes us through challenges that we would never face on our own. As we navigate the process of overcoming our struggles, faith has a way of reinforcing our true identity and implores us to be a presence instead of being okay with being present. As faith continues to nudge us, if we comply, we find ourselves embracing, acclimating, and owning what God sees in us. This is how we begin to live again, by faithfully stepping out of the misery of existing and awakening our spirit to our truth that sheds God's light on our circumstances.

I was finally living again. All it took was having the faith to step up, and here I was being fulfilled by the life I had avoided since I arrived on campus. What we see lives in us and frames our perspective, which can be empowering or imprisoning. Because I had witnessed so many people fail at being an effective leader and witnessed the ridicule of the guys who tried to step up, I imprisoned who I knew myself to be because I could not see myself being the guy they would follow. When I allowed faith to lead me, the process of facing challenges re-framed my perspective as faith pushed me to new heights and awakened the leader I had locked away. Once I stepped to the front of the line, I never looked back, I never questioned myself, never felt out of place, and I no longer felt that void that comes with existing…I had my HeadDownPushing.

I was named team captain by my teammates prior to the season and named the offensive MVP at the end of the season. I did not make it to the NFL, but through faith, I changed my entire college experience by scratching the itch I had avoided the prior three years. My desire to be the leader at Baylor that I had been all my life was fulfilled. I experienced what it was like to see myself as He sees me. Is your faith alive and well or is it yet to be awakened? Are you living or existing? Don't just claim to be faithful, put your faith on display.

The journey brings about encounters with who we are becoming, who God sees us as, which begins the process of changing the way we think as His love and His message through our lives is revealed to us. The faith that pushes you into new things is the same faith that reassures His presence in the ups and downs and reveals His intentions through each experience, ultimately changing your perception. Jesus said, "The light of the body is the eye." He was referring to perspective, which starts internally and not externally. We look at things, people, and life in general based on personal experiences. Our eyes and mind respond to triggers based on the influence of our experiences, but in His will, we consider Him first, which overrides those triggers. Those natural reactions/behaviors of fear, uneasiness, intimidation, and inadequacy are all overridden by what His word has planted in our hearts...Him. Relationship invokes a confident humility or a humble courage to carry you forward when things appear unfavorable, because you move based on His plan as the priority and not your own selfish intent.

When you replace preference with purpose, your perception is completely different because your eyes, as Jesus informed, have a new perspective, through faith, where fear and inadequacy have turned into anticipation, excitement, and the boldness to be the message that God intended.

Chapter 3

HUMILITY

Acknowledging God First in All Things, Stripping Away Your Pride and Ego, Enabling Yourself to Receive Help, Seek Help, and Give of Yourself Without Looking for Anything in Return

Faith invokes an all-encompassing gratitude. Similar to the Agape love God has for us, an impregnable state of gratitude where we are grateful just because, not founded on or fueled by any external or internal influence. In this state, we are aware of negativity and positivity, but our focus remains on the fact that we decide if our circumstances will make us better or hold us back. Gratitude pushes you to acknowledge opportunity, appreciate opportunity, reflect on how unworthy you are to have opportunity, but accept you are a chosen vessel to seize the opportunity. One of the most important factors in how you see yourself is owning that you are a vessel. Knowing you are a vessel is critical, as being a vessel validates and reinforces assignment, capability, purpose, uniqueness, significance, and love. Relationship teaches us that you cannot accept being a vessel without accepting all that He has told you that you are in Him, which you could never earn. Jesus knew His assignment and was not swayed by the ways of the world. His understanding of who He was through His relationship with the

Father enabled Him to stay on task and serve at full capacity at all times. He understood the world would not understand Him and that would create enemies, but He did not let the actions of His enemies change His approach nor did He allow the lack of understanding of His followers to influence His decision-making. We must be like Jesus in that every moment of each day, we have to be humble enough to live for something bigger than us, own our role, knowing we will be ridiculed and questioned, but never allow outside influences to stop us from living on assignment.

Owning your role incites confidence, embraces your unfavorable circumstances/outcomes, seeks to uplift, and commits you to fulfillment through service. A vessel's primary focus is their assignment because being on assignment brings you to God's presence as He uses you to do His will, impacting your life and the lives of others. Nothing has humbled me more than knowing that God wants to and is using me as I am. Despite every reason I could identify as to why He should just forget about me, He still uses me, and the same is true for you. Every issue, fault, disease, disorder, and decision that you could list as to why you cannot, should not, or would not is exactly why God is going to use you. Those things that you have experienced, those things that make you…you, are what others gravitate to; they are how others identify with you and why God chose you. What you have been counting as a knock against you are all pieces of your significance. You tap into the immeasurable power you possess when you acknowledge and own the value that God sees in you, not the lies you have accepted as your truth. The humility and gratefulness that accompanies this revelation don't allow you to look down on someone's circumstances; they do the exact opposite in placing you in their shoes and imploring you to lead them to a better place.

Humility provides an empowering absolute truth if you are willing to accept ownership of your actions and your intent. Relationship is key in this process, as relationship redirects your focus to God's presence in your life instead of dwelling on negativity derived from comparing yourself to others or focusing on unfavorable aspects of your life that are out of your control. Humility reminds you where you have come from, where you are, and the promise that He has been and will be with you where you are headed. Humility's truth transforms your being by providing you a new perspective; this is why humility is so powerful. When I began to know His love, humility pushed me to look back at my life and do a self-assessment that enabled me to see the value in all experiences, whether favorable or unfavorable. Where my selfishness pushed me to focus on the negatives by reinforcing the fact that I did not get the results I wanted, I now could see the value those times contributed to my life. If you reassess what you thought were failures, trials, and hardships with a humble perspective, you will identify the growth, strength, and knowledge gained that your selfish perspective does not allow you to see or accept. Understanding the correlation of your intent, your actions or non-action, and the results (your circumstances) is empowering because this is where you discover the control you have on your life, which reinforces being grateful for every opportunity (especially the opportunity to serve). Free yourself from the burden of opposition that your selfish perspective dwells on by recognizing the endless opportunity life provides through embracing a humble perspective. Possessions can be a distraction as well regarding how we see the world and/or how we see ourselves in this world, but understanding the most valuable possessions come from within frees us from the burden of gain and fills us with gratitude and the determination to honor all that has been given to us that we could never afford.

Pride and Ego Make You Put Up Walls That Eventually Keep You Out

The walls you put up in your life are the walls that keep you out. This quote has two layers of interpretation. The first layer is the most obvious in that people seek and find the same fault in you that you seek and find in others. So if you happen to be looking down your nose at others because of their income, title at work, ethnicity, choice of dress, financial class, sex, etc., then you can expect someone above you, by your own standards, to do the same to you. This is inevitable because we reap what we sow (the energy we put out, we receive back). We all have different starting places; where or what we are born into is not our choice. Therefore, the progress we make cannot be measured by the same standard because what one has to overcome to go forward or be successful is immeasurable. Self-images, support systems, exposure, mental road maps, and positive influence vary from person to person, and the same can be said for the degree of difficulty of life's obstacles. It is more important to consider what we cannot see than what we see, as what we can see is a result or reflection of what we cannot see.

What we cannot see is where we find the second layer of interpretation. The mental space or realm that we operate in has a spiritual connection to those in the same space. Consequently, if you lack humility, you cannot connect to the people you should connect to because your interests and intent don't allow you to embrace the same perspective. You are either too arrogant, prideful, egotistical, or simply unaware of the value before you. On top of that, their interests and intent steer them away from you because your disposition, demeanor, and temperament represent everything they are against or do not agree with. A disconnection with thriving humble servants is detrimental, as God has placed people in and around your life to serve a greater purpose. Likeness in spirit and/or the light in your spirit compels them to draw near, urges them to sow into your life, and brings you to people who are waiting to open up doors for your ascension. Do you have walls up that keep you from seeing people? If so, your walls are why you are not seen. The value humility displays in you connects to people long before talent, but walls of pride and arrogance prevent others from seeing past the façade. The walls you built that keep you from seeing the true value in people hurt you, but the most pain will be in discovering those same walls prevented others from seeing your true value and made you fail to see opportunity where God positioned his people meant to help you.

Your greatest gifts are you and your time. You are your most valuable asset and one of your most valuable attributes is your ability to be shared. If you believe this to be true about yourself, then you cannot ignore the same about others. For a long time, I thought I needed millions of dollars, facilities, and unlimited resources to change lives. Then one day a friend took the time to tell me my online posts had impacted her life and she was sharing them with her child. I was dumbfounded because I couldn't fathom how my words meant to encourage and impact my friends on street corners resonated with a middle-aged Caucasian woman. It was in this moment, through her appreciation & gratefulness, I realized all I needed to start anything was me. The impact I had on their life was not due to anything I received or possessed; instead, the impact came from everything I had been through and everything God had placed in me. From that point forward, I have always tried to consider the source when I decide not to give of myself. Am I not doing so because my pride is in the way and I am fearful of how it will be received or is my ego preventing me from being true to myself? We all would like to deliver perfection in every effort, but that is simply not realistic. Pride and ego lead you to delaying or waiting because they steer your focus away from adding value to deploying or promoting gimmicks. The bells and whistles of gimmicks may display investment and even alter experience, but true value-add flows through our authentic truth. Our purest form of ourselves offers quirks that some may compare to what they consider faults in their own lives. As they witness greatness in you despite these quirks, the connection to themselves encourages them while reinforcing your significance to yourself and others who were in attendance. Authenticity is the only gimmick you need because being true to yourself enables you to own the lane created for you. No one can duplicate what makes you unique, and that alone sets you apart. When you put up walls, you miss the opportunity to increase your worth by not focusing on the value you bring to the lives of those you serve. Focus on adding value in your role, not what you can gain and remember authenticity connects, not gimmicks. Once you have added enough value, you will be overcompensated in the form of internal reward, money, recognition, investment, and opportunity.

When I began the process of tearing down walls in my life, I experienced that when you give purely…you receive, when you push pride aside…you get pushed forward, when you welcome all…doors open for you. Patient, considerate, attentive listener, judgment-free, encouraging, reaffirming—when I exhibited these qualities, I witnessed darkness disappear and light flow out from people. At the same time, I felt life erupt inside me, I felt His presence as His vessel. I know I am His vessel and my job is to be my best to be used by Him in and out of each day. So I first must be available to receive from everyone and give to everyone despite appearance, reputation, perception, and convenience. What is your assignment? Are you submitted or are you looking for a shortcut to benefit you? If you wish to move up, give up…give up your ego, tear down those prideful walls, and give of yourself to others.

When I was kid I used to be excited to have new things like any other child. I loved getting the new J's (Air Jordan Shoes), fresh new trendy clothes, bikes, and remote control cars. Over time as I met more people my peers began to use my parents as a weapon against me, finding ways to make me feel bad for what I had, even though I didn't rub it in their face intentionally. For many years I allowed those attacks to rob me of my confidence and push me to be more considerate of others than they were of me. Not saying being considerate is a bad thing, but we should never compromise ourselves to please others. In trying to please others, I was becoming a shell of myself as each time I deferred from my truth, I gave up a piece of me. When I dimmed my light so others could feel better about themselves, they had no regards for my spirit. In reaction to each time I felt mistreated, I would stack a log on my internal fire to be successful. It's nothing wrong with determination, but we can't let someone else's behavior alter our identity.

Ultimately I ran into two problems with how I was dealing with these experiences. My first problem was that the logs of anger, spite, and vengeance that I had tossed on my internal fire were becoming my identity. When we approach life through anger we shut down a large portion of our spirit that allows us to operate at full capacity. Rage blinds us from the big picture that we see when we put God first in order to prioritize our agenda of making others feel our wrath.

In 2010 when LeBron James left the Cleveland Cavaliers to team up with Dwyane Wade and Chris Bosh on the Miami Heat he was perceived as a villain to many because of the way he left and who he went to play with. In response to how others perceived him and treated him across the nation, by his own admission, he began to play the game angry. Passion and anger both incite a tenacity that is prevalent in our execution. The difference is passion is advantageous as it activates us, but anger blinds us by making us close-minded. When asked about losing the NBA finals, LeBron says he was not himself and that the plays he left on the court were out of character for him. After enduring one of the toughest experiences in his life, in losing the 2010-2011 NBA finals, LeBron dedicated the next season to getting back to being himself and playing with a fun-filled joyous spirit. In doing so he was named the 2011-2012 NBA Most Valuable Player (MVP) and led the Miami Heat to the NBA Championship. LeBron's focus on how others treated him cost him as he allowed their actions to alter his being. That humbling experience drove him to new heights once he tore down the walls of anger that previously held him back. The logs of inspiration that external sources provide should fuel us to turn our intensity up, but we have to be careful to not let them make us lose our focus/honor of God's will.

My second problem with my experiences was I allowed external influence to make me look at my greatest resource outside of God, my parents, as a knock against me versus embracing them as a blessing.

What is Your Message | Marques Roberts

Half way through the fall semester of my Redshirt Sophomore year my roommate and I decided we wanted to live off campus without consulting our coaching staff or any other advisors prior to signing our apartment leases. After the leases were finalized we went to our Director of Football Operations to get our housing records updated so our monthly stipend could be increased. At that moment he let us know the budget is set at the beginning of the semester and there was nothing he could do to have our checks updated. So here we were living off campus with an on campus stipend or income. We didn't have enough money to pay our bills on time so we would spend time each month with our electricity off. The house phone, because at that time we all had house phones for no reason, was cut off permanently along with the cable and after about a month or two my cell phone was completely off.

After my phone was off for a couple weeks, I remember waking up on Saturday morning thinking to myself that I'll probably be hearing from my mom soon. I laid down on the couch watching a VHS and 30 minutes later around 8 or 9AM I heard a knock on my door and I knew exactly who it was. "Hey dad, I figured you'd be coming" I said. "Yep you know your mama, here you go", he said as he handed me his phone. "You know she wasn't going to leave me alone until she heard your voice." "Hey Mama", I said. "Hey Marques, boy why haven't you called me", she asked. "My phone is off", I answered. "I know that, if you didn't have the money you know you should have let us know". You could have used your roommates phone and given me a call to let me know what was going on at least" she exclaimed. I didn't have the nerve to say my roommate wasn't around because the power hadn't been on so I said, "well we get paid again next week so I was just going to call you once I was able to get it turned back on". What, unh unh, no you weren't, that's too long," she let me know. I went on to explain our snafu with our stipend and she let me know she would take care of my phone from there on out. We talked a little more to figure out a plan for the phone and went back and forth enough for her to feel reassured that I was okay. After we hung up, my dad said, "Man you know better than that, all you have to do is let us know. That's what we're here for". Then he pulled out his wallet and gave me some cash and said, "Well you take care of yourself and don't do this anymore. Now let me get back on down this road because I have a few jobs to get done".

I laid back down on the couch after our goodbyes and began to question why I had not let them know my circumstances and why I felt bad about getting their help. When I thought about how they only wanted to help and take care of me I realized how much of a fool I had been. For the first time I truly understood how blessed I was to have them as my parents and that my perspective was hurting me more than it was helping me. This day taught me a lot about being helped and helping others from a pure place. I learned we all need help and the humility it takes to allow others to help you is just as significant as the humility it takes to help others. When we have not truly experienced help, we fail to understand how to help in regards to our spirit and approach. The last thing I had to accept was help is just as much about the giver as it is about the receiver. My parents were not looking for an award or celebration. They were just doing what they were supposed to do. They were passing on what had been instilled in them. It wasn't about money; it was about accountability to God for the role that had been entrusted to them. What they did to my spirit that day changed my life forever. I knew I could never pay them back for everything they've done and everything they are to me, so my way to pay them back became making my life count. Their actions pushed me to drop the pride and the anger to pursue success with new inspiration and new perspective. Experiences like these drench you in humility, forcing you to question your perspective and the source of your intent by asking you "Is it about you?" after revealing the true reasons why and how you do what you do.

Everyone Won't See the Good in You, but the Right People Will

When I did not make it to the NFL, my life came to a standstill. I did not know what to do because I did not invest time in any other area of my life outside of football. The world to Marques the man, not Marques the athlete, was foreign. I did not know where to turn, what questions to ask, or what I wanted to do. As soon as my lease was up in May, I left Waco and moved back to Luling, hoping for an opportunity to play football at the professional level. Coming back home was a very humbling experience, as my self-centeredness was right in my face as the source of many of my issues. The helplessness of your fate being in someone else's hands is a very uncomfortable feeling. Everywhere I went, adults and children asked me about the NFL, "Hey Marques, you going to any camps," "You gonna do any tryouts," "I heard you were going to the Bears," "I can't wait to see you play on Sunday." I usually smirked and then answered with the usual, "Thank you," "I appreciate that," "I'm waiting, but I should know soon," and shook my head as I walked away, loathing the fact that I had no control over my life in regard to football. I kept up a routine of working out, waiting, and avoiding people so I did not have to answer questions about the NFL for about 4 or 5 months. After a few failed try-outs and declined offers, I closed the door on football, but I had no idea what was next. During that period of waiting my dad "advised" me that I should get a job to keep some money in my pocket. Till this day I think he had me come work with Him doing some plumbing work and with his friend doing cement work in the middle of the summer to ensure I did not get comfortable. I can say it worked, because I'll take the short-lived soreness of a football game verses the state of soreness of that manual labor any day. After a couple months my dad got word of another opportunity that he had put in a word for me for. He gave me some information and told me to give them a call. Without any hesitation I did what was required of me and made my way in for the interview. This was my introduction to the fact that I had essentially no work experience, no internships, and no volunteer hours to display the value I could bring to a position. Lucky for me, experience was not a requirement and a day later I began working for a Security Camera company as a sales assistant. I learned a lot about sales, workplace culture, office politics, discipline, employer loyalty, the responsibility of leadership, knowing your worth, and controlling your own destiny. But as time passed, the job became more of a roadblock than it was a launching pad, as it aided me in ignoring and settling with the fact that my life was not moving forward. It did not take long for my mom to sense that I had no intention of taking control of my life and the distractions I had embraced, traveling, women, and alcohol had me headed down a path of self-destruction.

One evening she called me into her bedroom and I knew by her tone it was serious. With a look of exasperation, she said, "What are your plans? What are you going to do? Cause I'm not going to sit by and watch you throw your life away with your friends. I am not going to let you end up dead or in jail." I initially jumped on the defensive. "I'm not going to end up dead or in jail; I'm not out there like that…come on, Mama," I said, trying to avoid the bigger issue. She acknowledged my refute, stating, "You don't know what can happen to you out there," but she did not lose focus. Immediately she went back to the source of my issues, asking again, "Well, what are your plans because you have to do something." Now I could see the love in her eyes and feel the sincerity in her words. With my voice cracking and unable to look at her as I began my response, I said, "I don't know, I don't have no plans, I don't know what to do, and I don't know how," making eye contact as I displayed my vulnerability and helplessness. Feeling my sincerity she asked about what I had done to help myself first, asking if I had looked for jobs forty-five minutes away in Austin and what I may be interested in to start building a career. I had looked online, but I really had no clue of how to job search, what resources were available, or what I was even looking for. I don't remember her offering too much help with the job search process, but she told me I had to do something because my vacation was coming to an end (I had to get out of the house). I had no anger, bitterness, or pity for myself in that moment because it was what I needed to hear, but was not willing to face out of fear. She'd seen enough of my dwindling ambition and my passionless routine of heading nowhere. Knowing I was the only person who could save me she wasn't willing to support me delaying the process of turning my life around and I was grateful to have someone love me enough to tell me I needed to do more with myself.

Not long after our conversation a young lady, who years later became my wife, helped me get an interview for what I call "my first real job." In the first quarter of 2007, I moved to Houston to begin training. During my interview, I was completely transparent about my work history and used football as my reference point for most real-life scenarios I had to deal with as a leader, which I think my boss appreciated. She was supposed to send me to a facility across town, but she decided she wanted me to be on her team, for which I will be forever grateful. Her decision to keep me close to her allowed me to gain experience, exposure, and relationships that all continue to reward me to this day. Initially, I was excited just to be away from home and focused on doing whatever it took to be successful because I always believed that "what I did not do" cost me the opportunity to play in the NFL. But I had never applied that truth to my life beyond football, so this was my chance to change that narrative. Only I had not considered the culture shock I was about to endure in working for a major corporation.

Over the next four years, I was stripped of my pride, ego, and remaining false confidence. My name, a name that was respected in my hometown and at Baylor, meant absolutely nothing in Houston. I knew no one at church, I knew none of the socialites, I knew no one at work, and more importantly, no one knew me. While I was in Luling the distractions aided me in avoiding my truth, but being alone in Houston forced me to face myself. As my frustration began to grow, I realized that I unknowingly adopted the mindset of most young men whose athletic career comes to a surprising end—those who have nothing to show for the time invested and have not put any effort into other areas of their lives…I believed I was a nobody. Whether it is high school, college, or professional sports, a trade, or a career, when that thing you believe makes you "you" is no longer an option and you have no "Plan B," you will be lost. I was used to hearing/seeing guys dwelling on high school memories and dwindled opportunities after they quit or were kicked out of college, but I was the captain of my team, I was the offensive MVP, I had a college degree, I had experienced success on the next level. Still, our stories were the same because, without the game, we allowed ourselves to have no identity.

After letting go of football, my pride and ego pushed me into a vicious cycle of chasing ghosts, misinformed or misled ideals of "who I am" and "who I should be." I was lost and did not have the necessary insight or knowledge to address my issues. While I easily transferred hard work and teamwork into the office, I did not know how to transfer the leader from the field into the office. The confidence I had in myself as an athlete was not there for the young man away from the game. Joining the workforce, the learning curve of the new industry I was in, and being in a new city was very intimidating and overwhelming at times. This is normal for the transition I was going through, but no one informed me that this would happen. So in reaction to my circumstances, I suppressed my feelings, learned to manage the demands at work, and kept my bills paid. I had gone to Houston like I had gone to Baylor, ready to make an impact, but once again my self-perception would prevent me from rising to the occasion. To keep from being overwhelmed any further, I shifted my intent from excelling to survival, which led to being stuck in a state of survival for too long.

Looking back, I've since realized after being in Houston a few weeks, I was miserable, but I did not understand the source of my woes. This continued for a couple of years until I realized I was not happy with my life. The joy that I was missing made me look inward, and I knew the void I found was, once again, a result of the lack of God in me. So I began investing more time and effort into my relationship with Him. As that relationship grew, I invested more through prayer, reading the Bible, and listening to sermons on the radio as I drove to work. The information was enlightening and empowering, revealing that I once again had settled, and I was stuck. My reaction was to focus my effort on learning more about my industry, growing as a person, and working to get a new job, which happened in less than six months. Less than two months after starting the new job, I realized there was still a void, but I still could not explain what was eating me up. One day on my way to work, I listened to Dr. Tony Evans preach about calling, passion, and purpose. By the end of my ride to work, I knew what was missing…purpose. I started planning in that exact moment. I made a commitment to myself to get at least two years of leadership experience before even thinking of a new job, but to never again grow roots or be at the mercy of someone else. I refocused my energy outside of work into prioritizing the interest of others above my own searching for outlets to serve others wherever I could find them. I began to lead Sunday school lessons with the youth, volunteer for events at the church, and serving in any capacity from setting up to cleaning up at my friends' non-profit events. Renewed relationship gave me a humility that provided a peaceful clarity, which enabled me to understand the value of where I was. So I decided it was on me to soak up information not only to get where I wanted to be but also to believe in myself to be successful when I made it. I grew in relationship, I grew as a person, and I grew in knowledge of the healthcare industry as well. After a little over two years, I was prepared to seize the opportunity of stepping into a managerial role at a new job.

Ironically, even though my new job paid more, I was unsettled because, through serving others, I discovered my calling. Instead of jumping the gun by quitting my job to pursue my calling, I humbled myself and embraced the opportunity to serve the new group of people God had entrusted to me. This changed my whole experience at this employer because they embraced me as a vessel and reciprocated service by encouraging me to be the light I talked about burning in them (you receive what you give).

Later that fall, my wife and I attended a Christmas party sponsored by one of my employer's vendors and I ran into the Executive Vice President of the initial employer I had worked for. Seven years earlier, I had been a contractor in his department. We spoke minimally back then; we never had any meaningful conversations I can recall, but we did have respectful greetings and small talk. Our group was under one of his Directors, who never greeted me or even acknowledged me, for that matter. Knowing there was no relationship there, I really focused on doing quality work and engaging the staff to build a good relationship with the people my team worked with daily. Fast forward seven years and I was still in contact with a few.

That night I was led to start a conversation with him and he took over from there. "What are you up to now?" He asked. I replied, "I am a manager now and I've been there about four months." Then everything changed. "Is that right? Well, you make sure you take down my email and send me a message on Monday because I'm gonna give you a real damn job!" "Yes, sir, I will. No problem." Throughout the night he reminded me two or three more times to make sure I emailed him. I told my wife, "Wow, I never would have expected that." She asked, "What are you going to do?" I replied, "I'm gonna send him my damn email address Monday morning like he said." We laughed as we got in the car and drove home, reflecting on how much we enjoyed ourselves. Over the next six months, I reached out twice to follow up. After the second follow up, I was brought in for an interview with him and two other Vice Presidents that he worked directly with. As he walked me out of the office that day, I said, "Thanks for the opportunity." He replied, "No problem, son. Shit, you create your own opportunities. Now you take care of yourself, and great job today." His statement has never left me, "You create your own opportunity."

On the ride back to work, I thought back to when I first moved to Houston and how God had placed people in and around my life who noticed me. When I was worried about where I would be working, the Regional Director kept me under her watch, and her successor pushed me to stretch in my role. My next manager made sure I was exposed to information and being the mother away from home she is to me demanded I give my all because she wanted to see me winning. When I asked, "Do you have any openings?" she went directly to the Vice President and they brought me on their team. While I was there, they consistently mentioned possibilities in areas under him to keep me around. When I left, it was like leaving a family member more than an employer. After that, God blessed me to spend nine months under a group of completely different, but exceptional leaders. My direct superior was as transparent as she could be. She offered personal advice about minor details like engagement and body language while positively reinforcing I should never lose what makes me who I am. I was also mentored by her peer who previously held my position. She gave me tons of insight, introduced me to critical elements I was oblivious to, and provided more professional coaching for my personal growth. I was tremendously grateful for her effort and her time. She gave me tools and information that helped me be successful in my role.

However, she did offer a piece of advice I did not accept, which made me successful with my next employer. It started with advice about executive presence and how I carry myself. This was affirmed in her opinion because she didn't think I talked to one of my teams enough, but it was the team I talked to the most (I even wrote daily motivational quotes that we discussed in the pod that they reminded me about if I forgot. I also texted them the daily quotes for some time after I left). She thought I had no relationship with the other managers, but I was the only manager who made time to establish rapport with each individual on the management team. Everything she mentioned was based on assumption versus experience or investigation. What she was asking me to ask of myself felt like it was out of the box versus authentic.

While I know there is a way to coach presence, I also believe we all have a natural presence that grows and develops with time.

Where she saw a lack of presence, she ignored the impact I already had. After making the initial mistake of accepting the criticism, I eventually realized humility is not easily identified if you don't appreciate or honor it. The best leaders lift up, not peer down; true leaders meet people where they are. To be perceived as a possible executive based on presentation is flattering, but I would never sacrifice being approachable or transparent for my own personal gain. Some individuals go out of their way to appear to have an air of distinction that makes them seem arrogant or distant. I would rather exude a humility that enables me to engage, connect, and empower. I connected with employees throughout the department on various teams through interaction and reputation; I was well received and well respected by the other managers, and I had a great rapport with directors from other departments. She assumed based on glimpses as she passed by, but never really looked into what she did not see. If someone cannot see you or refuses to see what makes you special, then it may not be for them to see, especially if they don't know what to look for. Leaders come in no specific package that identifies their significance. To identify true leadership, you must turn your eyes from the person to the people they serve. True leadership is planted and grows through people. Anyone can give directions, but true leaders affect lives that affect more lives and so on and so forth. The last piece of treasure came from the recently promoted Vice President of the department. What she did with this portion of her own journey will always live with me. As she adjusted to her new role, personally and professionally, she sat her leadership team of directors and managers down and shared her experiences and offered us the tools she was using to be successful. I am not able to articulate the impact of this experience to this day, but the humility shown in her transparency and attempt to empower us made me want to work to be successful for me, but even more so for her.

After spending those ten months growing at my new employer, here I was standing in opportunity back where I first struggled with believing in myself. As I drove from the interview, I was filled with joy and I was grateful that I held on faithfully to my vision. After I received an offer a few days later, I realized God had taught me a life lesson that would live with me forever. If you do what you are supposed to do for the right reason, the person you wish would notice may not, but the right person will. None of these people had to open their door, take time out for me, or even consider giving me an opportunity, but they did. I was once again working with my first employer within the group I was only previously contracted with. Even more ironic was that I was hired by the boss of the boss of the director who did not give me the time of day.

Are you working and growing, putting your best effort forth despite how you feel about your situation and/or the people around you? Are you focused on getting attention or letting your impact bring attention to you? We always hear that it is not about what you know, but who you know. Humility teaches you that it is not about who you know, but who knows you. Be grateful for all opportunities and make the most of them because you never know who is learning about you.

Humility Introduces You to Your Greatness and Then Tests Your Humility

I am definitely not who I want to be, but, over time, I have learned part of our assignment is to spend our lives not becoming who we want to be, but who He desires us to be. Relationship has taught me what makes me significant is already there—I just had to be faithful enough to walk in it. In life, we create our own identities through labels given from family and friends, roles we take on, family history in our communities, perception of how others see us, and expectations others have of us. As I previously stated, when first I arrived to Houston my perspective was from a place of complete insecurity. In my mind, others saw me as low value and expendable because that is how I saw myself without my "reputation".

I had to realize that the smile that lit up a room, the personality that intrigued others, the confidence to not follow the group, the peace to be quiet, the wherewithal of people's tendencies (discernment), the heart that desired to give were all still intact. These blessings I was born with were not merely characteristics of Marques Roberts the athlete, they are gifts of Marques Roberts the vessel. What instinct, attributes, or personality traits have you lost sight of or stopped embracing? Society suggests why we can't or aren't and we don't question society or ourselves; we just box ourselves in mentally, living within the confines of stereotypes, fear, pride, hate, prejudice, and lack of confidence. What box are you in and how long do you plan to live (operate/think) and dream within the parameters of "what your life should like" instead of discovering what you can create with your life?

Life's outside influences mold and shape our minds when "Me" and "Them" are our priority, but when we humble ourselves and allow purpose to be our biggest influence, we begin to see that God's perfect will has and continues to mold and shape our lives. Ask yourself how humble you have been in your life, how often do you leave God or a greater purpose out, who have you looked past because they did not fit the description, who did you disregard because of the title they did not have, or what did you pass up because you could not see yourself being successful?

Humility reinforces the significance of opportunity through relationship by reminding us of the magnitude of the gift that opportunity is. When we truly appreciate and honor that gift, we figuratively die for it daily. To paraphrase Jesus, "To follow me, you must first deny yourself daily (die), then embrace the specific burden you personally endure by following me." He then goes on to say everyone refusing to embrace that burden moves further and further away from who He called them to be. They let the things of the world be their greatest influence, but those who choose to die find themselves. This means those who choose to ignore the lies of the world they live in experience their true significance/greatness by bearing the burden they have embraced in following Him.

In dying, spiritually, we are free to be the most honest, pure, and innocent form of ourselves. Second, we mentally embrace the burden of following and reflecting Christ by releasing the cancers of this world that exist in us in the form of limits we have accepted from others, mental blocks we created on our own, fear, arrogance, pride, and selfishness that kills who God created by choking out our confidence, faith, humility, vision, freedom, innocence, selflessness, and joy. Lastly, we embrace that the results or execution in opportunity speak so loudly that we physically sell out every fiber of our being for God to breakthrough. The repetition of this process humbles us through revelation and the impact experienced in our lives and the lives of those He uses us to influence. In many cases, we want to believe we are built for the burden, but we are not. The burden prepares us for the next burden or obstacle by teaching us that we are not created to survive or overcome on our own. This is why we must walk in humility and be grateful for all that we endure because as owners of assignments we are responsible to be present with our gifts in full capacity for the next opportunity that God coaches, supports, pulls, pushes, lifts, and loves us through.

If you get sidetracked by focusing on what you are not doing or what you have not done, receive that as a sign that your life or intent is all about you. This lets us know that our issue isn't our circumstances, our issue is our perspective. Our perspective is derived from our sources of influence and any time we're comparing ourselves, standards and selfishness, not humility, serve as the basis for our perspective. Outside influences impact us so much at an early age that our unassuming thoughts are lessened or corrupted as we learn to compare ourselves with others focusing on what we or they lack. Over time, without the right guidance, the focus of lack shifts from toys and snacks to possessions and status; blinding us of our true worth. We get so caught up in things and what they imply that we look to other lost people for validation and degrade ourselves daily by comparing ourselves to superficial standards that lack any substance. Humility moves us from ungratefully comparing ourselves to others to honoring the opportunity to be able to work exactly where we are with what we have. Focusing on your wants makes you miss what God is doing according to His desire for your life. What you think you want may be why you are facing a specific opportunity (your lack of humility may make you see this as an obstacle right now) for God to use you to give away exactly what you need to learn of its true value. An arrogant, selfish disposition prevents you from recognizing the significance of your own needs so God sometimes allows you to go through an experience that forces you to see how you've failed to acknowledge that need. We all remember being humbled by being stripped down, but when we are experiencing Him through relationship sometimes He humbles us by using us to speak to us.

Humility enables you to witness your greatness while keeping you grounded. As you work toward executing your goals as a willing vessel you encounter pieces of you that you could only discover in the unknown (The mental & physical space that exists beyond your established comfort zone). The impact of what you experience changes your perspective, because when God lifts you up as a person, despite the outcome, you begin to analyze all that you cost yourself by not facing the challenges life has continuously presented. At the same time you become overwhelmed with humility knowing you were not alone. These experiences push you to work harder, be more available to impact others, and build a confident peace in your spirit with who you are in all situations. This confidence not only empowers you to be comfortable with who you are, but also what you do, and the value you add.

In my new role, I noticed a change in my disposition and perspective because my focus was no longer on validation, approval, or my insecurities that robbed me of energy I should have been using to perform/execute at my highest level. At first, my new perspective was intimidating because key indicators of character and intent became clearer in dealing with my peers and leadership. I knew what I saw, but I still took the long route to learning to trust my intuition. In conversations, I noticed individuals would religiously seek to validate themselves and/or undercut others. On top of that, I saw how leaders responded to employees who focused on deliverables versus employees who focused on stroking their ego. Don't get me wrong, we all should take time out to build a rapport with everyone on our teams, but things like quality, deadlines, and consistency should not be sacrificed to do so. The job of the leader is to create an environment where all personality types can flourish, but egos often get in the way, so I had to adjust my behavior to maintain rapport but let my work/impact speak for me. When you see peers or teammates spending extra time with leadership and appear to be doing well, your confidence and humility are tested. You are challenged with staying true to yourself and trusting your ability or veering off course to seek affirmation to provide a sense of comfort. Because I had the least experience, said the least throughout the day, and had the least in common with my peers and leadership, I questioned my value and my leader's confidence in me. Instead of focusing on bringing my best to the position, I tried to fit in or do things to get their approval. Frustration and anxiety caused by my focus struck a chord with how I allowed insecurities and assumptions to misguide me before. In those moments I learned I am responsible for being bold enough to be myself and not micromanaging the progression of work relationships because I could not find a place of comfort where I had to suppress the real me, which only made my interaction with others more uncomfortable. I was all too familiar with the stress of trying to fit in, so I turned away from that urge and let the relationships grow organically. After I refocused and prioritized adding value instead of garnering attention, I was able to add elements to our group that made us a stronger team. We all have faced situations where we know our expertise, talent, or insight could make a huge impact or has made a huge impact, but we create issues for ourselves because we stop focusing on adding and begin focusing on receiving. Instead of being humbled to be in a position to contribute, I found myself in my own way driven by selfish intent and insecurity. When I got out of my own way and focused on executing/delivering, more of me showed up and revealed what I could not see. As our bond grew, my boss took the time to nurture what I could not see and push me toward what she believed I could be, which gave me glimpses into greatness within myself I did not know existed.

Being new or uninformed is unsettling in any setting, but it is a part of the process of progress and growth. If you wish to keep progressing in your personal life and/or your career, there will always be some sentiment of new happening in your life. New relationships, new roles, new territory, new responsibilities, new perspective, new location, new processes, etc. but with each new opportunity, the stability of your mental transition becomes a lot less rocky if you allow yourself to grow through the process each time you have to adapt/adjust to new circumstances. There are so many elements that impact us in transitions that if you are honest with yourself you'll see how, in the past, you weren't truly in control of circumstances like you thought you were. Whether it was frustration, intimidation, fear, hurt, envy, or anger you allowed what you felt in your circumstances to dictate how you functioned versus taking control and bringing your best you to the experience. Some of you may be experiencing the frustrations of navigating something new right now and one of the biggest emotional mistakes you can make in these moments is comparisons. Comparing yourself and your circumstances to others is a dangerous place to be in because comparisons remove you (your faith, your principals, your experience, your vision, your intent, your investment, your passion, your joy) and replace them with what you see as your lack. You ignore what God has entrusted to you, as you lose sight of who you are in Him and where you are headed. This is why we witness so many people crash and burn, because they leave the purpose journey to join a rat race with someone with different end goals.

As we entered college a few of my childhood friends and associates began to make a lot of money hustling in the streets. The majority of them never threw it in my face; in fact, they actually looked out for me because we were so used to being broke as none of us had jobs. They also respected the fact that I wasn't jumping into something just because they were. I stayed true to the person they knew me to be so them letting me be me felt like encouragement to keep doing the right thing. This doesn't mean that's how they treated each other though and being a part of that environment had more impact on my thinking than I would've ever thought. As an athlete, you do not get paid if you do not go pro so for years I watched and listened to them compare girls, cars, speakers, rims, money, and almost any other materialistic object you can think of. I knew I could not compete because I did not have a job or sell drugs, so I did not even get into those matches, but I would think to myself how one day I wanted stuff that would allow me to shut the conversation down. What I didn't realize was I was already living it through my football stipend and Pell Grant as I was chasing those things when I did have a little money. For instance, I had to have the newest phone, real diamond earrings (because everyone had fake earrings), and expensive exclusive clothes to wear out (because someone may wear the same thing if I bought the cheap items). I even purchased a bumper kit for my car, knowing I am not a car person. In the end, I lost an earring I still had to pay for, grew not to like the clothes, broke my phones, and was unable to pay off the cost for the bumper kit that I never saw. Regardless of the outcome, I always felt like I got the short-end of the stick and I never felt like any of the purchases gave me the sense of accomplishment I was seeking. It took time, but I learned I cannot beat someone to where I am not headed. As long as it was their game, their intent, and their end-goal, I could never be on top and more importantly I would never be fulfilled. I had to ask myself who am I, what is competing and/or comparing costing me, where do I want to be, and what should my days look like to get there? When I was able to answer those questions, I knew I had to stay in my lane. Regardless of how far behind I felt or what anyone thought of me in my current circumstances, I had to learn to be content with where I was as I worked toward where I knew I belonged. I don't blame my friends for my mistakes. They showed me they honored me, but someone's honor for you means nothing if you don't honor yourself. You can't run their race and reach your goals; your prideful need to keep up or distorted desire for validation only misleads you into a race where you'll never find your pace, reach your milestones, or be fulfilled, because the race is not yours. Over time, running my race brought me a beautiful wife, invaluable knowledge, a Bachelor's degree, a Master's degree, a new house, beautiful children, multiple promotions, new cars, a quadrupled income, vacations out of the country, and countless invaluable experiences. Where I was headed, nothing on that list was on my radar, but changing my focus to owning my lane has rewarded me beyond my wildest imagination.

There is no competition or opponent more important than the competition with the opponent you see in the mirror each morning. You may or may not win those competitions with your peers, but what is the point if the winning cost you more than it rewarded you. If you ever decide to compete with that internal opponent, the possibilities are endless. Keep your humble confidence and stay faithful to what you know God has shown you. You will become discouraged, uncomfortable, and impatient, and each time you do, check your intent and your direction. As you continue to move forward and step into new things, remember the overwhelming reward you have experienced in humbly committing to running your race and how much time you wasted each time you let your insecurities get you out of your lane. The right person will recognize your greatness and guide you, assist you, or redirect you, so don't long to be seen; long to execute to the best of your ability. Your humility will be tested over and over, but stay the course, as you can only make the impact you are capable of making by being in your lane and being the vessel God called you to be.

Chapter 4

FOCUS

Being So Aware of God's Will That You Recognize Noise, Both Internal and External, But You Do Not Permit it to Make Your Vision Unclear

Growing up, I did not know the true meaning and significance of focus, and I was blind to the impact that our focus has on our lives each day. I always had dreams early on, but as time passed those dreams did not always translate to my day-to-day life. Over time, life has taught me that the dream is not simply an end goal; the dream is alive in us. We can suppress it, kill it, or bring the dream to life. We often hear the saying, "Chase your dreams." However, it is misleading because it implies the dream is elusive or something you reach over time. But the truth is you catch the dream the moment you make up your mind it is yours and enable the dream to order your steps. We don't catch dreams; we live dreams. If we see the dream, we cannot afford not to see the required commitment and effort to live it, or the reality of the cost of the dream may overwhelm us. This is what makes focus so powerful and impactful when working to bring our dreams to fruition. My journey taught me that we must embrace two levels of focus, an overall focus (vision) and a daily task-to-task focus. Our overall vision serves as a GPS or regulatory body, by setting a destination, revealing requirements for us to get to that destination, and then reminding us when we have lost direction. Our day-to-day focus serves as blinders that keep internal and external distractions off our radar to stay true to ourselves and the vision. The influence of our vision sets our focus each day. Being in tune with what we want and what that looks like encourages us to give less time to or stay away from certain areas, negative atmospheres, people with no focus, and misguided thoughts because we know they come with energy and distractions that deter our progression. We don't just wake up and assume this, but as we live, we understand how our bad decisions led to unfavorable outcomes. When we look at those decisions, we do ourselves a disservice by lying and trying to limit the incidents or pointing fingers at others. We must own the truth that our undesirable outcomes are a byproduct of the life we are living. If the results are not what you want or are not aligned with where you believe your life should be headed, then it is up to you to do something about it.

Day-to-day or task-to-task focus is not a conscious thought or effort—it is a state of being. In this state, we become so engaged or in tune with our vision that we deliberately seek information, work, energy, and company that push us closer to bringing our vision to fruition. We find ourselves in a state of submission because we must be obedient to the requirements of our vision, unmoved by what is taking place in the superficial world around us, as we are consumed with execution.

Take a moment to think back to any project, accomplishment, or huge change you had to adjust to. Letting go was just as critical to the success of the new endeavor as picking up was. It is critical to learn to let go because if we are focused on what was, who we were, or where we aren't, then we cannot give what is required of us to master what is and who we are becoming exactly where we are. Anytime we step into new territory, we are equipped internally to deal with what will be thrown at us. It is our job to identify what tools or skills we need to deploy to stabilize our situation and then figure out what steps we need to take to make our imprint or take things to the next level. This may sound straightforward or simple, but the complexities of the journey to making our imprint require deliberate focus and intent. New challenges, new responsibility, or any life changes, for that matter, are always accompanied by an emotional struggle. The new personalities, new atmosphere, new culture, and new expectations are all elements that have impacted all of us at one point or another. While they are all real, they are not all bad. What happens, though, is the discomfort caused by these factors pushes us to focus on our state, our feelings, and the source instead of focusing on our tasks/responsibilities, ultimately leading us to underachievement. It is exactly right here where we must let go of the emotions and focus on owning our ability to be successful in our new circumstances. To avoid routinely being misled by our insecurities on our way to failure, we must let go of our emotions. Letting go enables us to regain composure, have clarity of the vision, and redirect our focus instead of validating why we cannot be successful or finding a way to lose.

Think about the emotional rollercoasters you have experienced when circumstances were intimidating. The vulnerability of the unknown makes us uncomfortable, leading us to put up a wall of protection to avoid exposure, run in fear, use anger to attack, or use humor/sarcasm to deflect attention away from dealing with our real issue. When emotions are in control, we get in our own way by forfeiting our day-to-day focus, making us vulnerable to distractions that we attract or seek. Some people put out negative energy because of their unwillingness to deal with not feeling equipped and they have no problem attracting others who agree with any form of deflecting fault. We see this often on Social Media when someone posts one-sided inflammatory statements/perspectives with no context. As others add likes and comments to display solidarity the submitters use the feedback to validate their emotions instead of addressing the source.

Some of us seek to escape or numb our pain through family, work, drugs, alcohol, sex, video games, etc. so we don't have to think about the fact that we are not willing to get out of our own way. These are just a few of the distractions we agree with in favor of challenging ourselves to meet the requirements of our vision. There are many more that we enlist and/or attract because the work on the other side is either not appealing or not an option.

It's one thing to not be excited about working through your emotions, but to be unaware of the problems that your emotions cause is another level of problematic. Most people don't actively discuss or delve into dealing with emotions as a normal part of growing up so the acts of fleeing or avoiding are seen as normal instead of problematic in many cases. We simply normalize bad habits instead seeking to disrupt these behavioral patterns. This leads to individuals living at a disadvantage due to an emotional instability that hinders them from learning to overcome being intimidated and/or overwhelmed. This is critical because the day-to-day focus continually unlocks hope, but that hope fades when we can't see ourselves where we want to be because we don't know how to ask and give more of ourselves where we are.

It is tough to accept that we must give more and even learn to give more, but there are many people who are willing to trust someone to teach them this information. And on the other side there are those who are completely closed off to exploring outside their norms. Some of these people have taken on this identity of being a loner, which is true in some circumstances, but too many individuals are just using this label to mask their fear of challenging themselves beyond their learned behaviors. Shutting down or closing off is how they operate, because all they know is safety and misery. They don't know what it's like to be exposed and joyous because the pain and/or negativity they experienced from going outside of their comfort zone is what was thrown in their face until the positivity and insight of themselves no longer existed.

What others think is often an underlying factor in the motivation or influence of our actions. Whether it's family, peers, or complete strangers, more than we like to admit or are even aware of, the opinions of others affect our decisions. Looking back, I noticed it seemed like many people have found the courage to live with the results of their decisions despite what others think, while others stay chained to their fear of "what if." As I dug deeper, I understood that more people than I assumed are affected by what others think. For instance, sometimes the nature of what someone does or what they've achieved/attained makes us assume they are past caring about what others think, but if we talked to many of these individuals we'd find their circumstances are due to them feeling they should be exactly where they are. This sounds like it supports my point, but if where they see themselves is a reflection of what the world has taught them through learned behaviors, stereotypes, and self-imposed limitations versus them going outside of themselves to create the life they desire, then they actually haven't embodied the level of focus that we assumed.

This is not a knock against anyone's life, this is only evidence of the power of perspective and influence as well as inferior thinking, lack of exposure, and the many other factors that alter our belief of where we belong. You have to ask yourself how comfortable you've been based on the path you accepted or how uncomfortable you've been based on the path you've created to find your truth. Because the truth is as long as we feel we belong, life takes us wherever we desire because our actions match our beliefs. When we believe we belong, what others think becomes non-existent (as it always should be) and nothing can prevent us from attaining all we can from our circumstances whether it is being the best athlete, the best actor/actress, being the best truck driver, becoming an RN, becoming a physician, selling the most drugs, taking over a farm, being the best stripper, or even building our own business. It doesn't matter what the goal is or where the bar is set, if we feel like it's where we belong, we make it happen. It's only when we reach the point of stretching, where we have to ask more of ourselves as an individual, that we question our ability. Those places or people where our vision brings us to that ask for something from us that is unfamiliar or unknown so we are forced to choose facts or truth, limits or faith, and substance versus appearance.

What most of us don't know is, in these instances, we are confronting ourselves and struggling with deciding on the fleeting comfort of focusing on how others see us or the faithful peace of focusing on the internal/external progress of bringing our vision to fruition. People pleasing or faking it is commonplace in today's world of social media where we are celebrated for simply appearing to have it all. The problem with faking it is at some point the person has to match up with the perception and without the process the person can't deliver. Appearance garners assumption and substance garners belief or trust. Even though you should not seek validation, when you are of substance, the difference you make with your presence cannot be ignored. Substance encourages others to invest in you or believe in you because they agree with what you represent, while appearance leaves people wondering if you can be counted on because you lack the evidence of investment. Appearance cannot sell the experience, progression, humility, and confidence that are ingrained when gaining substance. Focus on being and becoming instead of being seen because when you seek attention, you end up with attention you don't want.

Where There Is No Vision, the People Perish

Yesterday's, today's, and tomorrow's leaders all have something in common, and that is vision. Whether we are examining bold entrepreneurs like Gary Vaynerchuk, Sean Carter (Jay-Z), radical leaders like T. D. Jakes, Joel Osteen, Steven Furtick, Malcolm X, Carl Lentz, or culture-shifting leaders like Martin Luther King Jr., Former NBA commissioner David Stern, Steve Jobs, or Jeff Bezos they invest in the life of their vision, which, in turn, continues to set the course for their lives. For the life of your vision, it is critical that you not only believe in your vision but also honor your vision, be loyal to your vision, submit to your vision, and protect your vision. Before anyone else buys in, you must sell out. Your actions bring your vision to life in the eyes and the spirit of others. Your investment, your commitment, your dedication, your will, your faith, your determination on display day in and day out fuels the people around you. The environment you create by pouring your life into what you believe in and those around you triggers them to do the same, and this is passed down to create so much value in the lives of others that you are rewarded with buy-in, alignment, investment, and loyalty in the form of service, references, inquiries, or whatever form of support/recompense people feel in their heart because of your contribution to their life. Understand this is a simple snapshot of the influential power of your day-to-day focus. You create something in others when they experience your message that is pounded into their being through your being, with only the intent of giving your best to them and your vision daily.

In many other scenarios, people in leadership roles give up or simply plateau as they rely on tradition for sustainability instead of being led by their vision. Instead of leaning on other's strengths as they guide the entity or team, they prioritize protecting their pride and validating their presence out of fear of losing their position or not feeling capable of facing the challenge of the unknown. This can be witnessed from city to city or town when visiting smaller churches that are full of tradition and absent of vision. Vision is ambitious, innovative, inviting, challenging, intimidating, exciting, and progressive. Vision is not redundant, reluctant, stagnate, closed-off, and unambitious. Many of these churches are victims of their own routine and conformity; afraid of stepping outside of their comfort zone to become, instead they choose to be satisfied with existing as they are. If you are not working toward your vision, then you are working to survive or sustain. Survival causes teams to defeat themselves from the inside out because they work against each other instead of working with each other. When in survival mode, departments, teams, and cliques prioritize personal gain or praise over the people they serve and each other. Individuals in business have these same struggles, as we see small business owners or other entrepreneurs get frustrated by lack of support or no instant return. But lack of support should be expected and seeking instant return should be avoided instead of sought out. Survival mode derives a "what's in it for me" mentality versus a "how can I best serve you" mentality. This ultimately chips away at the passion, fun, confidence, trust, commitment, and loyalty associated with the team, business, or service until they are gone.

Too many people are seeking a quick come up versus investing in the long game of optimizing how they can add value. Everything I've witnessed come fast, I've watched it go fast: from drug money to oil money, street fame to internet fame, new fads to internet trends. The difference in the outliers in each of these categories is the foundation built prior to the "overnight success." Either existing content kept the interest or sustained an entity until they created something new to engage their audience or they were so invested, experienced, and prepared by the journey that they were able to respond to their success almost instantaneously, unlike their counterparts, who became overwhelmed or distracted by newfound success. When the goal is to make money, become famous, or go viral, a lack of substance is exposed in the downfall. For your vision to come to life, you must be obedient to what the vision requires of you in effort, consistency, and intent.

Obedience creates a discipline that becomes the foundation to build your future on. I truly believe our vision of ourselves comes from God, but we taint it with selfishness and vanity that misleads us down a path of self-destruction where we prioritize serving our ego, greed, and pride that disrupts our ability to make sound decisions. For instance, when we seek how we can best serve ourselves by doing the least amount of work, in the least time, with a mediocre effort, we are not being obedient. When we set out to impress others instead of being true to ourselves, we lose the essence of what the journey creates in us that others gravitate to. This is why you can't let status become a priority over the process of building, because you can never catch the reputation you are chasing, but you can build a tremendous reputation that you won't be able to explain, by submitting yourself to your vision. In service, we give of ourselves looking for no return. In selfishness, we give to receive. This starts by putting our energy into trying to control what we can't. Then we stress ourselves out by chasing optic to optic or opportunity to opportunity hoping to gain enough approval, money to look good for another week, or social capital, never pausing to consider the value of substance. The same nothing it takes to put on the façade for others is the same nothing that does not hold up when tough times occur, but the investment in building and working on your vision stands the test of time through a solid foundation of faith and discipline.

We create feelings/emotions in others through our selfless acts, which others digest, causing them to form their own interpretation of the experience. This is how you build a reputation. If you can ignore the noise, you will discover there is a peace in being true to yourself because you don't have to bear the burden of pleasing others. Too many people forsake the solitude of the process for the calamity of affirmation by aiming to impress. If we chase, we relinquish control and allow that which we are pursuing to control our actions. When we allow self-serving desires to direct our decision-making, we drive ourselves into an internal state of war. The materialistic and egotistical things we chase cause restlessness in our spirit and chaos in our thoughts that distract us from the peace to be had in the process, as the process is reassuring; our intent either fuels that peace, which fuels our focus, or when misplaced, makes that same peace non-existent.

Many of my friends and I experienced the allure of being "the man," whether it came through the role of being the top athlete in town, living the street life, or both. For most of us, the greatest allure was that of the athlete, because in our community, nobody had it better than the guy who ruled the field, court, or both. Many saw the respect he received, the love everyone gave him, and how he inspired others, but I saw even more. I saw how he was revered in all social circles and accepted by other classes/races that normally gave young African American men the cold shoulder. On the other hand, I also saw that the person was absent from the persona and who people catered to had nothing to do with the individual. Witnessing this pushed me to navigate my journey delicately because of all the attention associated with being in that position. It was tough for me to understand why so many people opted to go the street route instead of steering clear of what ultimately became the downfall of those that came before us. I constantly wondered what made people think, "I want to do what they are doing" when they knew they would end up dead or in jail before graduating. Later after facing intersections in my own life, I understood that our choices are not because of what we see, but because of what we don't see.

In my youth, I did not understand the impact of perspective on the decisions we made. With time exposure changed how I saw myself, which, in turn, expanded my vision, so aiming for anything less than where I believed I should be was unsettling to me. Starting around 11 or 12, I watched my older brother go to a virtually empty weight room religiously every day of every summer when he was in high school on his way to earning a scholarship. When I made it to high school and began to make those same lonely trips to the weight room. I never thought about not getting a scholarship. I studied everyone who did and who didn't learning what impacted their situation and what I needed to do to avoid the same fate. I had multiple setbacks like losing eligibility because of failing grades and underperforming due to a lack of confidence, but ultimately knowing where I wanted to be would redirect my path.

Growing up hearing stories of local guys like Troy Lampkin shooting shots from near half-court with no three-point line, Willis Mackey running touchdowns in front of Barry Switzer of 80 and 85 yards back to back because someone jumped off-sides the first time, Roger Mackey slipping before running a 10.4 100m dash, or Billy Jack leaving strawberries on your face from passes you never saw coming validated that being a Luling success was possible. But the stories of Bo Jackson, Deion Sanders, Jerry Rice, and Michael Jordan pushed me to think beyond. I not only wanted a Luling story but a story the world could tell. The requirements of my vision and my hunger guided my work ethic every summer. When my friends were sleeping in during the summer, I was working out; when they were playing around in the evening, I was practicing; while others did not take the class seriously, I made sure I made the grades that would make me eligible for Division 1. I worked on making it every day. I did not work to have a local success story; I was working to get out. Four years after my brother signed a full scholarship to play football at Sam Houston State University, I signed a letter of intent for a full scholarship to play football at Baylor University.

For the next few years, my belief and commitment to my vision would be challenged. I knew what it took to set myself apart and achieve what few had achieved in high school, but lack of self-confidence, conflict with authoritative figures, the unknown, and the minimal support that many of us face in college was overwhelming, especially since this portion of my college experience was unexpected. To add to my frustration, I had never dealt with many of the issues I was facing, so I really did not know what I was experiencing that made me feel helpless and depressed. I had watched firsthand what it would take to get out of Luling, but once I got to college I had no reference point for what it would take to get to the NFL. I faced a couple of rough patches early on in practice, but they were limited to football technicalities, so I knew how to deal with that process, which led to me doing some great things in a matter of weeks. Then when things went in a direction I was not prepared for, without a thought, I resorted to a lifestyle I had avoided for years because that was familiar to me. Instead of choosing to face the challenge, I retreated to my comfort zone. I had reached my point, similar to what my peers in Luling experienced, where I could not see me being successful so instead of fighting I decided to fold.

Looking back, I realize I let myself and others get in the way of doing what was required of me. I lost focus because the unfamiliar obstacles and emotions were a part of tough times that changed my perspective, limiting the vision I had for myself. Tough times don't mean we need to change our vision; tough times mean we need to intensify our focus. To get through these moments, we must put our heads down in the work to avoid all external and internal noise trying to pull our attention away from doing the day-to-day work that builds us up and/or makes us better. This work is intimidating, frustrating, confusing, and sometimes very painful, but there is no way around it. Part of the process of growing through the work is learning to focus on improving in stamina, in strength, knowledge, and patience instead of focusing on the suffering, lost time, unfairness, and isolation.

Up to this point I acted from a basis of what others had done so I never took the time to learn and invest in the significance of Marques. I relied solely on my talent within the game because I believed I was as good as any of those who came before me in my own way. Now life brought me to a point where it was past time to move past dreams and idolizing to visualizing, working, and executing. It was time to live the dream based on who my investment had shown me to be in Him, but my perspective limited what I gained from my investment. When I should have been studying myself to become more aware of my strengths and weaknesses I was more focused on not messing up and getting through the day without conflict. When I should have been investing more in my relationship with God to understand who I was in Him, I was trying to convince myself of who I was based on what others had not done. My focus was rooted in the internal noise of who I wasn't and the way things weren't instead of being derived from who I was in Him and where my vision was guiding me.

Sometimes the noise of the dream is so loud that we forget the solitude that the work provides. I did not need to run to my comfort zone to avoid the noise. I needed to run to the work to create peace. I needed to invest in who I am in Him, not who I'm not based on the standards of the world. Whatever you have faced or are facing may be shrinking your vision right now. Don't do what I did and create more chaos by fleeing. Create your own peace in the middle of the storm by believing in your significance and refocusing on the day to day by pouring your energy into the work, ignoring all internal and external negativity. Focus on the work your vision has brought you to until the work settles the noise and your new confidence lifts your head up to your new perspective.

It's Not What They're Saying; It's What You're Saying

In today's culture, it is commonplace to acknowledge our "haters" and what they cannot stop us from doing. But the real opposition that impacts our lives comes from within. It was never what someone else said or did that stopped your progression. It was what you believed yourself not to be that stopped you before you got started or derailed you in the process because you could not see you being successful. Instead of addressing our thoughts and their source, we put on a façade of confidence and accomplishment to save face among our peers. Our concern for others has shifted from caring about what others think to manipulating the thoughts of others through social media. We have become so conscious of others in our daily routines that risking our reputation or representation is not an option. The irony is that many people, in what are considered unfavorable circumstances, glorify or boast "how bad/rough life has been" "how they are from the bottom" or "how he/she wouldn't last where I'm from", but are also the first to turn away from betting on themselves outside of their comfort zone to get out of their situation because of the fear of looking and feeling like a fool. In other words, they are saying "I would rather look proud in my misery than look foolish pursuing my destiny." This way of thinking and living is inherited and promoted among many African Americans, not knowing the choice of not betting on yourself suggests I am scared of failure and don't believe in myself enough to take a chance outside of my comfort zone. No one would readily admit to this, but then again, how would you know this is your issue if it is all you have ever known?

Operating based on what we believe ourselves to be is reflected in our relationships, friends, career, and service. Because we don't see much in ourselves, we cut off the vision and the uneasiness it invokes and welcome the ease of avoiding being tested. This space of comfort is a safe haven from the challenges and requirements of your vision, where we must endure the pain of failure and defeat. You may remember some of your first failures or mishaps and the pain you experienced, including the embarrassment, negativity, and in many cases, the finality of the situation. We all had those experiences as adolescents, but as we grow, it is critical that we gain a new perspective on how to deal with failure because if we only recall those initial emotions and reactions, we close ourselves off to anything that could possibly assault our pride by tapping into those same emotions. The gift and the curse is that you may be protected, but prideful pain serves as a warning from our vision that we are on the wrong path; so ultimately saving our pride costs us bringing our vision to fruition.

There will never be a time that opposition does not exist. Before you consider any other source of influence, reflect on the story you have been telling yourself that hinders your growth and your progression. No one has ever spoken anything into my life that stopped me unless I agreed with them. Whether it was good or bad, I had to first give their presence, energy, actions, words, or thoughts permission to influence me. Granting permission is easiest to allow when it already exists. It is not tough to disregard what people are saying; it is tough to disregard the fact that you agree.

Heading into my senior year at Baylor, I hurt my knee a week prior to the beginning of fall camp (Two-a-day practice). I would be out for about three weeks total, meaning I would miss fall camp and the chance to solidify myself as one of our top offensive options heading into the season. Unbeknownst to me, our offense coordinator had already decided I was not a top option. I started my entire junior season and had one of the best spring seasons among the receivers. The thing was one of the new coaching staff's transfers was the guy he wanted in my position. On the first day of camp, everyone went to the meeting rooms first and those of us who were injured went to get treatment. When I came into the meeting room, the depth chart was posted, and I was listed as second. I will never forget how I felt seeing that chart and feeling ready to go to work.

When the meeting was over, everyone filed out and my position coach let me know that he did not agree with that change and said we will get that taken care of, but my only response was, "Okay, Coach." I had no room to invest in what someone thought of me because I was fully invested in my ability to show that position was mine. I focused on getting healthy and taking every mental rep I could to give myself an advantage despite my situation. The person ahead of me had the skills and ability the offensive coordinator preferred, so he had been given the position; he had two weeks of work to solidify himself as the guy before I even suited up, and all I could think about every day was my next mental rep and when my cleats touched the grass for the first time.

After returning from a couple of weeks of rehab, I heard things like, "He took your position," "You should be with the first group." Then people asked, "Why are you with the second group?" But I simply went to work; I did not even ask if I had a chance to get my position back. I never invested any energy into the negativity; I just stayed the course of stating my case through my actions on the field. Once I got back on the field, I don't think I was back longer than a week or two before my place on the depth chart changed. In the prior seasons, I paid too much attention to the noise and my lack of focus showed up in my day-to-day execution. I allowed what I could not see in myself, what my teammates had to say, and the negativity of my position coach to push me into a place where my actions did not match my vision. At the end of my junior season, I set the vision and made my day-to-day focus match up with where I wanted to be. So when I was faced with adversity, I did not shy away from the challenges I faced over the next two years, because I knew what my alternative was. What they were saying no longer agreed with the story I was telling myself, so the negativity did not move me. I knew my investment in the offseason and the summer was not in vain, and when I showed up to practice, what I was saying to myself echoed in what displayed daily on the practice field.

Don't Let Where You Are Have More Influence On Your Decisions Than Where You're Headed

Once you understand you are on a journey and have established an overall focus, the daily process of becoming reflects the message of your life. Let's revisit a few stories and analyze how vision grounded in faith provided a path that my day to day focus drove me through to bring my vision to fruition.

Investing all your being into the smallest actions and transactions enables you to be fully aware of who you are in each moment of becoming. There is something to be learned or taught in all that you do and everyone you encounter, so it is critical that you are focused even when you are not aware you are being watched, because God uses your actions to minister to the hearts of others. Focus enables you to remain connected to God to operate freely and innocently as a servant of His will and not tentatively as a slave to a selfish agenda. One slip or lack of focus opens the door to lose that state of being. Everything from cleaning our homes, picking up a piece of trash in an aisle at work, holding doors in public, to courteous driving, exercising, hosting meetings, personal conversations, and greetings; as you move from task to task, your focus evolves from engaged intent to a free state of being where the peace of being in God's will rules your spirit, stripping your shoulders of an unjustified burden, welcoming your submission to being His vessel in all exchanges. The pureness of your spirit in this state connects on levels that we cannot explain, but what we know is that it leaves a mark—a mark that touches the lives of other individuals and incites a burning desire to become, to pursue whatever left that mark, so they can experience it for themselves and pass it on to others.

I lost track of where I wanted to be after my freshman year. There were so many obstacles constantly reminding me of their presence and my helplessness each day that instead of looking to work, I looked to just make it through the day. The more defeated I felt, the more I shied away from challenging myself until my intent completely shifted from being a presence to being content with being present. What I did not know was when the seed of vision is planted, the instinct to pursue flows from within. So if we are being disobedient in regard to facing the challenges our vision brings before us, then every day we wake up, we must face the internal struggle to turn away from the pursuit. This is why many athletes and/or entertainers end up miserable and depressed when onlookers assume we are having the time of our lives. Like everyone reading this book, I had a decision to make. Do I keep running from the challenge or stop and do the work required to be who I wanted to be? I decided that my goal of impacting others meant too much to me to leave that campus without giving the best of myself to my teammates, the community, the program, my hometown, my parents, my family, my friends, my coaches, and myself.

My situation was so difficult for me to deal with that I lost sight of where I was headed and almost lost my scholarship because I let where I was have more impact on my decisions than where I was headed. As tough a time as this was, I would not trade it because this period prepared me mentally for the challenges I faced after not making it to the NFL. When I came back to Luling from college, I had no clue what kind of career I wanted, and that lack of vision enabled me to slip back into a cycle of aimless content. If you feel you aren't about anything you'll do anything to make you feel like you are worth something. That was a scary place for me because I was my own worst enemy. The thing about my circumstances that kept me together was I knew who I wasn't so there were some lines I never considered crossing out of respect for myself and my parents, but not being sure of who I was made me vulnerable to myself.

What is Your Message | Marques Roberts

I don't know what home is like for you, but going back home for me meant if you saw me with 3 people, those 3 people had a pocket full of crack. If you saw me with 9 people, those 9 people had a pocket full of crack. Everybody was selling, sun up to sun down. I won't go into the ins and outs of our days, but I will say they were not very productive for me. I would go workout then basically spend my days/nights out with my friends while they maintained their normal routines. When I look back at this window of time, I realize that we must be in tune with our vision to make sure our actions are contributing to our journey and not robbing us of our time. When my dad suggested I needed to begin working that kept me out of the streets as much as I was, but it was not until I began to realize what I had been doing with my time that I got uncomfortable with my routine. As I spent less time on the block hanging out, the familiarity of my circumstances reminded me of Baylor and my decision prior to my senior season to not let my current situation be my story. Through reflecting over the years, I've learned that I can go numb to the world when I am determined to get something done or running from my truth. As far back as my childhood I can remember having to have things taken away or being forced to quit because I was determined to conquer/master whatever I put my mind to. During college, when I began running from my truth, the time I dedicated to being a student athlete allowed me to ignore my feelings about not being fulfilled. The fact that I was working towards the NFL also provided a false reality that I engulfed myself in because of everything the process masked in regards to my lack of confidence, lack of direction, and lack of love for myself. After college, next my story was, 'I am working out to be prepared when a NFL team calls", and after that my job as a camera salesman validated that I was doing something while it truly was only helping me avoid the fact that I was working towards nothing. You may be in an aimless routine right now that includes a job, sham, or excuse that you use to avoid what you aren't doing and where you aren't headed. Like me, own your truth that the situation you're in or the excuses you claim are a reflection of your lack of vision, a safety net for your unwillingness to take control of your life, and a roadblock for you being intentional about your life.

I moved to Houston physically after almost two years, but I did not move into a new mental space for another three years. My aimless content lasted for almost five years until I decided, "I am no longer allowing my life's journey to be dictated to me, and I am taking ownership of where I am headed." I ended up leaving my initial employer in Houston because of instability that constantly reminded me of my lack of control of my circumstances that I had just experienced through football. I was paid less in my new position but my focus was on the fact that I would get much more exposure and have the opportunity to gain a wealth of knowledge. Sometimes you may feel like your path is going backwards with the decisions you make, but you have to evaluate what is of more value to you and aligned with where you are headed. There was no room for growth where I was, but the investment in myself I made while I was there provided a bonus I could take wherever I went. Having value to add made me excited about the opportunity, but I also had more to learn which made me focus on becoming to get where I wanted to be. I had not felt like this since I arrived at college. The money I gave up in switching jobs was not life-changing, but the challenges of my new position would be accompanied with information and exposure that did have the power to change my life if I made the investment. In my first weeks of college my pain started with lack of investment in myself when I was afraid to believe in myself enough to step outside of what felt safe. Fast forward 11 years, in similar circumstances, I didn't even stop to consider my emotions because I knew my investment was driving towards my vision.

Prior to transitioning jobs my vision required that I enroll in a MBA program to help position myself for where I was headed. Not long after the fall semester began my wife let me know she was pregnant. This was the most scary and intimidating news I'd heard to date because, in my mind, I trying to figure out how I was going to take care of my family. Now, there was no time for figuring it out; figuring it would have to happen as I made it happen in regards to providing. With the culmination of pressure from my new job, school, and parenthood I flipped a mental switch that had not been turned on since I played football. I worked overtime relentlessly (5/5:30 am to 8/9 pm) every day, so much that I completely lost track of time, as my wife had to let me know that it had been three months and not the three weeks I thought had passed since I took a break. The news that my first child was to be born shifted my focus from "need to" to "have to." I was no longer up for settling or being unintentional. Realistically, I always knew my wife could take care of herself, but the news of being responsible for another life hit me in my core and changed me forever. I thought about where my decisions had brought me versus being where He wanted me to be and how that impacted my family. Knowing no place could be better, I had to make a shift in my life so that everything I did added to positioning myself where God wanted me to be.

Time became a sensitive topic because I saw time as the one asset we cannot recoup. I became a very intentional person, calculated in decision-making and laser-focused in execution. I paid attention to the details of the work I was doing and even though I may not have had the alluring title, I knew the work was valuable to potential employers. I did not shy away from any roles or duties. I was wholly submitted to the work because I knew it was essential for where I was headed. My perspective was the work is available, my boss is pushing me, and I need it, so it only made sense to capitalize instead of seeing it as being taken advantage of, or as an extra burden. I did not think of the work as a task. I saw the work as part of the process that was building me up for my next endeavor. I understood how the exposure to upper management would impact how I saw myself going forward, and I knew the value it added on paper (to my resume) as a potential candidate. In a little over six months, I became a supervisor, and I gave myself two years to learn what I needed to become a manager. In less than three years, I move to my third place of employment to become a manager, making twice the salary and four times as much as I made when I began working. My vision had come to pass, but it took committing to doing the work to get where I wanted to be and not showing up looking to avoid getting uncomfortable. I was not focused on how I looked to others or what they thought of me. Adding to me was my priority because I knew I could be confident in my investment. I knew I could not trick anyone into believing I was a good candidate. I had to do the work so that who I knew I had become spoke for me before I ever opened my mouth.

As I navigated the process of career advancement, I learned in order to gain value, you must add value, and you start adding by giving value away. You may be wondering, "What do I have to give?" Start by giving of yourself and your time. There should not be a task that you see as too small or as beneath you. There should not be a person in the building that is not worth greeting or giving your time. I did not set my sights on what I wanted, I focused on where I could lend of myself to my peers, my leadership, and the team I had been entrusted. Everything I gave to the workplace came back with add-ons that I was able to share and/or take with me. In most cases it was the add-ons that continue to help me to this day. One of which was learning the importance of knowing where you don't want to be and what you don't want to do. Knowing what I did not want to do made it easier to know what path I should be on and the experience I needed to be able to add value in the capacity I desired. I also learned that if you're not going, you're not growing. A lot of us at work expect the work, our employer, or our direct superior to ensure we are growing, but the truth is we have to make it a point to go. Meaning we have to be intentional in seeking out the information, the resources, and the exposure to build ourselves up so that we become long before we arrive.

The new position was ideal for experience, raised expectations, getting out of my comfort zone, accountability, career advancement, and salary for my growing family. I was forced to stretch, I was forced to get uncomfortable, I was forced to take ownership, I was forced to be the face of the department, and I was forced to be the voice of reason within the department. I had to instill confidence in the individuals on my teams, I had to instill confidence in my teams regarding my ability, I was challenged with taking on a new role and building trust in my leadership by displaying my ability while being trained by someone who felt they deserved my position. The attacks against me and the questions arising from the false accusations pushed me to heighten my focus on execution. I also turned this into an opportunity to trust God to reveal the person I was and not lose myself in the process of making others feel comfortable in my ability while my trainer planted seeds of doubt. I previously mentioned how, in this managerial role, I received invaluable coaching, mentorship, exposure, and relationships, but I knew this was not where I ultimately wanted to be. I honored and revered the opportunity to pour myself into my team members, but I knew I wanted to be a part of a team where I could be an individual contributor. I had spent the previous 3 years supervising, coaching, learning, and growing, and I was truly grateful for what I learned, but the new job was confirmation that that type of work was not of my preference as it was not fulfilling and did not give me the opportunity to utilize some of my best qualities that would benefit the employer. After my experience at my previous employer, I knew I had to be patient and once again channel my energy into now for what's next, but I was not excited about it. What did help keep me on track was the peace I had because I felt like I was where He wanted me to be, so I was willing to submit to the newest requirement of where I was headed instead of focusing on how much I did not favor where I was. You never know when your moment is coming or which moment creates the opportunity for "the moment," so you must treat every opportunity as "the moment" so your best is all you know to give when you find yourself in "the moment." When we don't take advantage by giving our all in our opportunities, we hurt ourselves by not becoming, which leaves us unable to identify the next opportunity or unprepared for it. You don't get an opportunity then try to display you are capable. You get the opportunity because you modeled the behavior of someone who is more than capable. Every time you push yourself to your limits you see more of what He has placed in you and more of what challenging yourself is building. I encourage you to get exposed, learn, grow, gain confidence, and never shy away from what you become attracted to or what you attract in the process. In fact, learn to embrace where your curiosity and passion lies, invest in your talent and strengths in that area, and be a savage in every opportunity that comes your way. This is vision, this is focus, this is knowing where you're not headed, this is not letting your circumstances stall your progress, this is becoming, this is…HeadDownPushing.

His Vision Is Always Bigger Than You

I always tried to make my past make sense, but there are so many nuances to our journey that each time we look back, the process of becoming provides more insight for the purpose, power, and value of all we went through, preparing us for where we are headed. Football has been invaluable to me years beyond the game, from entering the workplace, becoming a speaker, and as an author. While the time I spent playing was wonderful, it was not until after the game was long gone that I understood my selfish influence on my vision. I was able to turn my story around at Baylor when I began to focus on being true to myself by being a leader. While my efforts to leave Baylor in a better place than it was when I came were a positive influence, the source of my intent for the NFL was selfish. The game got all of me and my teammates were able to benefit from that, but they should have gotten more of me, which is what happens when our intent is misguided. My intent for the NFL was to get rich, be famous, and be "That Guy," so my investment did not align with God's vision because instead of prioritizing serving Him, I prioritized serving myself. So when I left college, I carried the same intent into every gimmick, job, and get-rich-quick scheme I got involved with until I became exhausted with falling short. Time and humility forced me to understand the value of service and giving; and how much more they did for me than anything I have ever physically possessed. The more I gave, the more I gained until life placed me in a position to maximize my passion to encourage, motivate, and activate others to take ownership of their own lives.

I was just looking to serve others, not gain anything, and I found myself speaking in front of audiences. I set out to make everyone around me better people and employees, and I found myself writing about it. I set out to leave something better than I found it and those who I impacted became the flame of the phoenix for the Baylor University Football Program. Obedience in intent, effort, and consistency bring His vision to fruition. Some may feel and look successful to others on the outside, but true success overflows with reward internally. It was not until I set my focus on serving others that I felt true reward, and over time, the value of reward versus award began to shift in my life. This shift created a new capacity for me to give and receive. Our day-to-day focus on being secondary to our service opens up avenues that we could not conceive. As we grow in relationship, we experience His ability to do above and beyond with our willingness to be used, which reinforces the service first mentality. Through the journey of seeking His will, our selfish, prideful, distorted perspective is removed and we gain more clarity for His vision for our lives. We become more determined and committed to enduring, fighting, growing, and being obedient to the requirements of His vision so we can continue to be used. If the vision comes from Him, our goal must be the day-to-day process of submitting ourselves to the work that builds who He sees not what we refuse to see. Many people are willing to do that work, but few do. The question isn't can you—it is will you? This process of becoming has to shift from being seen as work to being seen as the part of the vision that it truly is. The vision is yours as soon as you decide to direct your life to possess it. In the same instance your focus must shift from pursuing the vision to living the vision. In pursuing the vision we seek to manipulate the vision to be what we want it to be, but in seeking to live His vision we learn becoming requires your obedience to the vision, because the vision won't submit to you.

Chapter 5

COURAGE

The Strength and Mental Fortitude to Remain Steadfast to Your Purpose in the Face of Your Fears

Courage is how we recreate culture in the environment we live in and how we reconstruct the internal belief system from which we operate. Our lives are made up of instances of us choosing to settle or not settle for our circumstances and accepting or not accepting our circumstances as truth in the face of challenges. We all have the instinct that tells us there is more on the other side of our obstacles which urges us to seek more. However, the risk of what we see as a great failure or disappointment often prevents us from challenging ourselves to face the odds. Instead, we turn to our safety nets to guard our pride and ego, disregarding our purpose and responsibility to our assignment.

Everyone has conscious and unconscious safety nets they resort to, especially when faced with challenges. We retreat to these safety nets to either avoid our challenges and accountability or dabble in them without facing scrutiny. Safety nets are useful in being slow to speak and making informed decisions, but they can only provide a limited amount of protection in the process of living your dreams, as true progress requires that we embrace the vulnerability of life without the safety net.

Safety nets are hard to identify without self-awareness because our safety net tactics are hidden in the routines we embrace, derived from our perception of ourselves. Most of these routines include validating issues, which range from obsolete details to absolute show-stoppers, to reinforce why a plan will not work or simply to delay moving forward until another issue can be identified. Whether it is a lie or fact, we choose to hold on to our safety to avoid dealing with ourselves in the face of our opposition. This passive avoidance often leads to nothing ever happening as the individual is seeking the perfect opportunity, but true doers know the perfect time does not exist. Others settle; they may act, but their actions are never outside their comfort zone. The unknown factors are so overwhelming that they never pull the trigger without the assurance that they will not fail. True vulnerability is giving your best effort in your challenges despite the unknown. We gain insight through this experience, which makes us unsettled in the spirit when we go back to the norm because we know life has more in store. Being unsettled pushes us to keep working, this results in progression that provides confidence. Confidence sparks the courage to go fight for our 'more' that life has reserved for us.

When you recognize your safety net tendencies, you have to stop yourself from feeling overwhelmed, feeling defeated, holding back, or quitting. Use this moment of truth to make sound decisions, not decisions based on emotions. A decision should be made with the intent of moving beyond your comfort zone. To progress, it is critical to identify your safety nets because when you cast that safety net you create room for questioning yourself and your ability because safety nets are held together by disbelief. When you are not wholly committed mentally a single thought or mention of opposition is enough to incite fear that causes you to believe you are incapable of overcoming your obstacles, leaving you stuck in limbo or paralyzed in doubt.

What is Your Message | Marques Roberts

In the spring of 2000, I spent the entire 2 weeks leading up to the Texas High school State Championship Track Meet with a safety net in place. I was one of 8 qualifiers in the 3A division in the 110m hurdles. Prior to the meet, I saw that my qualifying time was not in the top third of the finalists, so I instantly began preparing to lose. Each day of practice leading up to the meet, all I could think about was how far the other runners would be out in front of me because they were faster sprinters. My mind was made up that I would be so far behind I could only hope I did not look a fool because the qualifying times I saw suggested there was no way I could win. Leading up to the race, I never stopped myself and said, "Focus on you, despite what the circumstances may suggest. Focus on bringing your best and living with the results, knowing you left it all on the track." Because I did not believe I could win, I turned to a safety net. I created a mental space that made it okay to not just lose, but okay to not give my best effort. Among my friends, I poked fun at myself about being in a race with the elite and not having a chance. I would say, "Man I'm just trying not to get embarrassed out here." Earning a medal was out of the question in my mind. I even said, "I'm out of place. I'm a football player on my way to Baylor University; I'm not no track dude." Ironically, this was more evidence for me to believe in myself not a validation of my fear.

On the day of the meet, before I walked down to the field to warm-up, I told my friends, "Let me go get ready and try to not get blown out too bad." This was my way of continuing to spread that safety net, creating an environment of no expectations around me so I did not have to take ownership of not being okay with not being first. After I began to warm up, I started feeling comfortable and becoming more eager to see what the other runners really had to offer. It was go time, now or never, but I then noticed that at this point where I was normally locked in on my race, my safety net was questioning things that had nothing to do with what I could control. This close to the gun, there was no place for doubt; it was too late.

"Runners to your mark" called the starter as my heart pounded. I tuned out what I could and focused in on this moment because I always owned the start of my races. We all lined up in our lanes across the track, stepped up to the starting line and stepped into the starting blocks. The next sound was a quick "set" and not long after my hips rose and paused in my starting position. Pow! The starter's gun blasted, and I was the first out of the blocks, which I, ironically, expected, but the distance was surprising as I felt like I created separation over the first hurdle. Then my safety net kicked in. I began looking for the other runners in my peripheral as I cleared the second hurdle, because my safety net would not let me believe I belonged in front. The lack of concentration caused me to hit the next hurdle, something I never did, making me lose the lead I started with. Normally in the races I believed I could win, my focus was on running my race to perfection, but my safety net caused me to be distracted on the biggest stage.

As the race continued, I was still in the top group, to my surprise, because according to my safety net, they should have been pulling away. Since I was running based on how I thought the race should go instead of focusing on running my best race, I could not physically outdistance or outperform my mental restrictions. No matter what I did physically, mentally I could not overcome myself. My lack of focus caused me to hit another hurdle, and I dropped back a few places to get into my "rightful" position. After falling back, you would think I would just finish the race and be glad to have that over with, but my thought was, "To have hit two hurdles, I'm not too far back. I need to run my race." So I locked in, but it was too late at this point because we were at the end and I did not have the turnover (sprint speed) to catch up with the leaders. I skimmed one last hurdle and ended up finishing in fifth place full of disappointment and regret for the race I ran due to my mental approach. I was excited that I could compete with the best in Texas but full of regret that I would never have another opportunity to put my best foot forward against them on this stage.

My safety net not only protected me but also restricted me. That experience taught me to be aware of my obstacles but not allow them to influence how I see myself. I also learned that the torture of regret is far worse than the pain of losing. Who knows what would have happened if I had the courage to prepare to run my best race leading up to the track meet? Who knows what would happen if you have the courage to run your best race every day in life despite what your obstacles suggest?

Safety nets originate in our thinking, become a part of our being, and then show up in our actions. It is not enough for you to just show up or be present. If your mind is not fully engaged, it will reflect in your actions. For example, toddlers in church are present physically, but the tablets, cell phones, talking, sleeping, and staring behind the pew indicate they are absent mentally. It is time to be courageous enough to get rid of your safety net(s) and see what life has in store for you. You will not know what you are capable of until you are courageous enough to be great with no strings attached. This means no reassurance of success, no regard for the odds you are facing, and no fear of failure. It is past time for no more regrets; respect yourself enough to empty your tank in the preparation and execution of every opportunity because life rarely offers more than one chance to be your best.

Your Problem Is Not Your Circumstances Your Problem Is Your Perception of Yourself In Your Circumstances

Ambition is powerful, but many of us lack ambition today due to lack of exposure, lack of positive influence, lack of confidence, and lack of support. To be ambitious is intimidating or burdensome in many cultures and communities because it is synonymous with being defiant. This is why it is so important to have courage. When no one understands or believes in your vision, it will take courage to pursue your vision in the face of opposition.

Historically, most people stick to what they know and don't venture into or open up to new things. Whether it is going to college, picking up your parent's trade/business, working where everyone else does, doing odd jobs, choosing not to work or selling drugs with your friends or relatives; the influence of culture implies expectations and places limits on your abilities. These limits become a part of us in how we see ourselves and how we approach life because these limits tell us who we are, what we are capable of, and what we are worth. As a result, our toughest obstacles are internalized. In fulfilling our ambition, we are forced to go against what has become natural; we must unlearn behaviors and change our internal conversations, starting with the way we think. This is where we introduce courage because courage is not introduced until we meet opposition.

Courage is often misleading because of what the actions we associate courage with imply. When we see people do something we admire with confidence and passion, we automatically assume they don't share the same fears or concerns that stop us. These assumptions are not the source of our issues; they are a byproduct of the inferiority complex we have embraced. Instead of seeking why they are able, we validate why we are not able. Instead of building ourselves up, we tear ourselves down, diminishing our courage to face our obstacles. This process of tearing yourself down, in the wrong circumstances or around the wrong people, turns into a cycle until there is no need for validation because you begin to identify yourself as inferior.

The celebrities and others who we admire have similar fears and endure internal opposition we are not aware of because they have different perspectives and experiences. The difference is they, unlike many others, have learned to not accept or have managed to stop the cycle of inferiority and embody the courage to do it anyway. They live from that source of determination created by their experiences instead of being led by fear.

When you avoid the challenges of life and never step up, you exclude yourself from experiences that establish the routine of being courageous. Facing your fears or moving on despite threats becomes second nature when you stop trying to avoid opposition and start expecting opposition. Expecting opposition prepares you to respond to obstacles and not react as you have in the past. Reacting is negative in that we give control to our circumstances in the face of our opposition, but responding is positive because we then take ownership of our circumstances in the face of opposition.

Fear actually becomes a tool to your advantage when you learn to embrace it. Instead of retreating to your comfort zone after talking yourself out of challenges, you begin to use fear to optimize and make the most out of your situation because you want to be your best despite the threats you have considered. Fear drives you to prepare, teaches you to expect the unexpected, and reminds you to be okay with the fact that nothing is perfect. Where do you lack courage? Do you try to mask your fear or avoid challenges altogether? Your courage is internal, waiting to be discovered, waiting to be unleashed into the world you have shied away from. It is time to discontinue the routine of living in fear and go in spite of…Do it anyway!

Are You the Journey or What the Journey Created?

The journey of life consists of peaks and valleys. The work in between those peaks and valleys molds and shapes us for the challenges we face as we go forward. A component in continued success or progression as you move forward is the courage to embrace the growth from the work and leave behind the negativity of any burden, pain, or perceived failure.

Countless internal and external factors fuel us throughout our journeys. The stigma that black girls don't belong in tennis for Venus and Serena; being drafted 199th in the 6th round for Tom Brady; or the early career struggles that include being homeless for comedians/actors Steve Harvey, Tiffany Haddish, and Kevin Hart are all examples of fuel. The key is to channel the energy created in the process into fueling your work ethic and determination (your passion), not allowing the energy to fuel your emotions and take control of your thoughts and actions.

I have never forgotten the days of my freshman year in high school when I had attitude problems of my own, but refused to just fall in line with the toxic culture the seniors created. I remember being told by one senior in basketball practice, "You'll never be shit" and by another during football season, "You'll never be like your brother." To the first I had no reply, I just decided to become so great that he realized he was wrong and had to eat the figurative "shit" he felt I would never become. And to the second guy in the locker room, I replied, "I'm not trying to be," which left him frozen and dumbfounded. I thought about those words all the time in High School and used them as fuel. Their words only made me more determined to leave my own mark, as my brother had obviously left his. They just missed the mark, they were so consumed with self-promotion and self-preservation that they failed to grasp what had been passed down to them. Instead of taking their fear and insecurities out on me, they should've pulled me closer to get what they could from me because I had the talent to make their teams better and more importantly they could've planted seeds in me to pass down to the guys following me. Instead they counted me out and because of what I saw in them I was determined to be nothing like them and more determined to become exactly what they failed to see.

Using past experiences as fuel keeps us aware, aligned, and determined, but allowing the energy or emotions from the experiences to rule leads to misguided intent and poor decision-making. I could've easily used their words as an excuse to start a fight or say something even more demeaning, but I took that energy and applied it to my effort in working towards something bigger. When we learn to manage the energy of our experiences, we are able to fuel the courage it takes to face any obstacles or opposition to come.

When I was bullied during my childhood, I would be attacked for reasons like having a big head, having working parents, hanging around different races, dressing different, being black, being smart, and many other reasons. When you get bullied, you never want to face those emotions again, so you do things to try staying off the bully's radar. As a result, I stayed away from many people so I wouldn't have to deal with them. I did have a few friends I was comfortable with, but there were only a few I felt I could be unapologetically me around. Just before middle school, I made a friend whose situation felt very similar to mine…scared of (respected) his parents, had friends of all races, was good in sports, had to be respectful, had to make good grades, and was expected to stay out of trouble. We never discussed our feelings, but our friendship represented freedom to me because we did not have to be guarded in each other's presence. This feeling of no pressure was rare and welcoming. The freedom to laugh, ask questions, or turn right when everyone went left without being judged was relieving and empowering.

The problem was these feelings were reserved for a very limited space in my life, causing me to feel constantly at opposition or guarded. I did not know how to be comfortably me in many scenarios, because I felt I was not good enough as myself or I was scared to make others uncomfortable even though their actions suggested they had no regard for my feelings. I had a lot of what I would call associates as we moved into middle school, but there was always this level of anxiety because I never felt I could be true to myself. As we moved into high school, I gained more confidence in myself through being a successful athlete so I became less concerned with how others felt. I was also taller and stronger, so a lot of the bullying stopped, but I did not hold a grudge or seek to get even. Instead of hurting them physically, I wanted to make them regret their close-mindedness toward me and people like me. I wanted to prove their stereotypes wrong!

As my relationships evolved over the years, I never forgot how the bullies or negative people made me feel or how I felt toward them. For a while, I considered my interactions with these people my fault so I carried it as my burden. This led to me being guarded because of the pain I felt. As time passed and I saw the same people mistreat person after person, I realized how they treated me was not my fault. In fact, how they treated me had nothing to do with me; it was a reflection of how they felt about themselves. This did not make me think less of them, but it made me think I should care a lot less about what negative people had to say. What was more important was creating new conversations with myself because I had allowed their thoughts to influence how I saw me. These new feelings/beliefs gave me more fuel to believe in myself, keep doing what I felt was right, and never be less of me based on other people's opinions. I missed out on numerous experiences trying to please others who did not care about me. Now those missed opportunities serve as fuel, because when you don't have the courage to live as the true you, you don't get that time back.

Sports became my freedom because I did not have to be guarded or a lesser version of myself in the athletic arena. They were a refuge from all the anxiety and complexities of dealing with people, whether it was in a game, practice, or offseason training. My friend and I pushed each other through fearless competition every day. Whether it was, tough battles in basketball, playmaking in football or going at it on the track, in our eyes 2nd place was last place. There was no scrutiny for striving to be our best and no care for what others thought about it. We could be vulnerable and have no conscience. No one was required to fit in; in fact, you were rewarded for standing out. We did not have to live someone else's limits, because settling was not an option.

With time, sports taught me that some of my perceived weaknesses were actually strengths: my willingness to accept everyone, my willingness to show up despite the elephant in the room, and my willingness to not settle for my circumstances. Do you have a place of refuge, a place where you can be yourself with no regard? If so, how much of yourself do you reserve for this safe place versus introducing the real you to other areas of your life? It's on you to allow your instincts to lead you to speak, walk away, support, or be quiet. You know the moments that you let pass you by because of your fears…I can't speak to your specific circumstances, but I can tell you about the sweaty palms, rising heart rate, warmth in your chest that makes you sweat, the tension that makes you as tiff as a statue, and the voice in your head that gets louder and louder the closer you get to breaking through. When the anxiety creeps in your faith has to be louder than the doubt and you have to refuse fear with every ounce of your being to trust what you've seen in your safe place because it's real. Those areas where we are most free are empowering and rewarding, but we lessen their significance when we limit the person we discover to this sacred area of our lives. Share that person with the world and in that niche you shied away from because you were unsure, unfamiliar, and did not think you had what it takes. The truth is you have something to add. It is your responsibility to have the courage to change your circumstances now and display the power we all possess within to overcome our internal and external obstacles.

I mentioned before that after about a year on Baylor campus, I experienced bitterness, selfishness, and carelessness which derived from a lack of self-confidence. Since I was outside my community of Luling, where there were expectations of me, I decided I could be less accountable for how I represented myself since there was no precedent set for me. No one knew my ambition, my heart, or where I came from. No one knew my parent's reputation, and none of that mattered, because nothing would speak louder than my actions. Everything was face value. Ignoring expectations freed me of a portion of that burden (because we all have expectations of our own that should be higher than any external source), but because I did not believe in myself, there was no bigger influence on my decisions than my fear of the unknown direction of my life. In my eyes, my presence was irrelevant, which added to the level of inferiority I already embraced. I was intimidated by my surroundings, so I hid my fear by replacing it with a chip on my shoulder. Prior to college, I was always empathetic, but I was still mistreated and/or underappreciated. Initially, I felt the same way at Baylor because we were at the age where tough was cool to guys and the girls were attracted to the bad guys. Seeing this, because I lacked courage, I decided to express the thoughts, behaviors, and disposition I had suppressed or turned away from my entire life. I told myself being too nice was a sign of weakness that would make me a target. On top of that, the ridicule you receive for going against the group to do the right thing is a powerful deterrent. Instead of owning my insecurities, I channeled the anger and bitterness of not being bold enough to be myself into that chip. I told myself that not being true to myself was no longer acceptable, even though I was not being myself. Instead of using my pain as an incentive to turn things around, I allowed it to drive me to inflict pain on others. I was rude, short-tempered, disrespectful, bitter, and arrogant. I had developed no feelings for the hurt I felt and the hurt I dished out. I enjoyed the freedom to say what was on my mind, but I often hated that it came at the expense of someone else's self-esteem and displayed the lack of respect I had for myself. As free as I felt at times I did not like who I had become, and my actions did nothing for the emotions I was experiencing. It did not take long to figure out that those chips on your shoulder get heavier if you seek retribution for something you gave away or something you could not control. I also realized the burden you add never sits well when you know the person who represents you is not you. In mistreating others and yourself you may think you are living free but you are only anchoring your being to the source of your pain hindering yourself from evolution. My wallowing in self-pity led to such destructive behavior that my state of being became unbearable. I was faced with closing my heart completely off to give myself away to self-destruction or committing to taking my life in another direction. Without a second thought I immediately let go of the pity, the fear, and the anger. I chose to find the remaining pieces of my shattered confidence I had given away to build myself up enough to find the courage to be me and live my truth.

Doing the right thing is a physical, mental, and spiritual burden because it is an assignment. The hurt, shame, anger, bitterness, and going cold was a result of not being courageous enough to fulfill my assignment. Instead of owning my role in my feelings, I took my pain out on others, which only added to the mental obstacles before me. I may have been attacked for being different or not conforming, but anything I lost like courage, joy, happiness, optimism, ambition, and confidence was because I gave it away. I realized I was living my valleys instead of learning from them. You see, it is easy to live your pain, but it takes courage to strive for more beyond your pain.

We often have a negative disposition toward new territory and the unknown because that is how we have been taught, directly and indirectly, to handle the uneasiness that accompanies them. I made the mistake of not being optimistic about my new Baylor community because I was wearing the valleys of my childhood where I shied away instead of embracing the work it took to climb out of that mentality. I completely allowed how I saw myself in my circumstances to alter my being, something I can hardly stomach to this day, because the decisions I made were induced by fear and anger.

What pain are you holding that is costing yourself or others because of the steps you will not take? How much of your pain is self-inflicted? How much anger, frustration, and bitterness do you make others suffer through because you are not doing what you should? Have you allowed yourself to pick up past pain to deal with present issues? Release the pain and embrace what the pain taught you to discover inside yourself.

For most of my life, I identified myself by what I had been through instead of embodying what adversity built in me. Make it a point to revisit your valleys, but don't stop there. See the work, the resiliency, the revelation, the progression, and the victory you experienced as you made it out of the valleys. Bask in the moments of breaking through and what those moments felt like in your spirit because it is a crime not to own that identity. Dismissing the person you became as you fought through valley after valley and disregarding what you witnessed of yourself as you made your way through those dark places is something for people who don't believe in you to do. That work does not go away, that strength, that knowledge, that wisdom, and that humility all remain, but it takes the same courage you displayed to break through…to live as that person going forward.

You may make some people uncomfortable, but when they settle for being mediocre, it is not your concern. Don't you dare allow their discomfort to stop you from being true to yourself.

When you decide to make being bold a habit, everything that was once an obstacle assists in you seeing/feeling the source of whatever pushed you to not believe in yourself. That clarity helps make you aware of how you cope when faced with adversity. Anyone who mistreated me may have been wrong, but that did not make it right for me to mistreat others. Mistreating others only made me like the people who mistreated me. The courage it takes to face yourself only prepares you for or introduces you to the courage you will need to overcome the internal/external obstacles to do God's will at the next turn.

Distance yourself from what you think others find admirable, trying to meet what has been determined as acceptable, and embrace the courage to let your most honest, unfiltered, and creative self-speak. Long before we ever have to open our mouths, we must be courageous enough to do what we know is right. That difference in our actions alone is loud. Whether you know it or not, the people around you hear the difference, see the difference, and feel the difference. Some gravitate toward it as it touches exactly what they are feeling, others only observe, and many oppose it when the difference makes them question themselves and they allow their insecurity to take control.

Don't Let the Fear of the Unknown Make You Experience the Pain of the Undone

Looking back at the time I spent at home after college, everyone around me was living a limited vision of themselves. It was not what they were chasing but who they believed themselves to be that drove their actions, and I was just the same. I raced back home to my comfort zone, settling in every aspect of life because I saw myself as a failure since I wasn't in the NFL. While at Baylor I experienced and overcame misery and settling. The strength my journey built was there, I just needed to learn to deploy it in a completely different area of life. Settling at this point was derived from similar circumstances such as lack of direction, confidence, and insight. The difference in the man versus the child was the experience of embracing the courage needed to face the unknown.

Every day, we allow circumstances to define us, but it is what we do despite our circumstances that truly define us. Coming to a place where courage was my only choice was the difference between me and many of my peers. While they had the courage to do what they felt they had to do, they were yet to have the moment where they bet on themselves. Betting on yourself takes a different type of courage because you have to overcome yourself and be willing to face your truth to change your circumstances. Challenging myself to step up and be me introduced me to the courage, sacrifice, and discipline required to change my life. So when I became uncomfortable with being uncomfortable my faith, vision, passion, determination and willingness drove my actions instead of my emotions, outside influences, or unfavorable circumstances.

Tapping back into what God placed in my spirit showed me this was something I had left in my childhood that I was missing. He was revealing more of me to myself and in finding His truth I found power. Little things that came instinctually like not doing what everyone was, wasn't cliché, it was who I was. I was uncomfortable not asking more of myself, so I was hiding because I had forgotten how to do so away from sports. I am only comfortable being crazy enough to live for what I want and the fact that I was accepting anything less hurt me to the core. The great thing is our senses can recall the pain of hurt and defeat. And when my senses felt defeat creeping into my spirit they also began to recall my actions that led up to me breaking free from the lies I attached myself to.

Breakthroughs, meaning anytime you disrupt your norms by courageously responding to life's challenges by asking more of yourself outside of your comfort zone, are meant to change our lives beyond a specific moment.

Experiencing breakthroughs free you from self-bondage if you do not restrict what you have witnessed to a specific area of your life. If we close off to what breakthroughs create in us or what we experience in breakthroughs we imprison ourselves to the limited perspective we have of who we are. Instead of letting life empower us to pursue more and experience more of His truth, we choose to accept life as it is. Accepting life versus directing life stifles us as we lose touch with the courage we embrace to make choices. Circumstances, similar to outcomes, push us to focus on what isn't. When we focus on results we lose sight of the true outlet that enables our power, which is choice. As people we don't gain power in results. It's when we make the choice to be courageous that our power through Him is revealed. When we experience that power it becomes our responsibility to be courageous enough to choose to get out of our own way in other areas of our lives.

Once I decided I wanted more from life, my actions drew a line in the sand as I did not compromise to fit in and that made others uncomfortable. I could not see it, but I was a threat. It wasn't notoriety, attention, or anything materialistic that I was threat to. I was threatening to expose the fact that they were not who they pretended to be. I was betting on myself in a way that was unfamiliar because I was all in on me. At the time I did not see this, I only knew I was finding my way in foreign territory. People who are threatened by you are not courageous enough to take the stand that you have; so they attack you and what you stand for, but you cannot afford to let them drag you down or place limits on your ability. They can literally sense your potential, so everything they do is to keep you down, influence other's perception of you, or not bring any additional attention to you because of the jealousy in their heart. When you are unwilling to compromise who you are, it's only those people who are mad at themselves for not doing the same thing that have a problem with you. This is okay because when you draw that line in the sand, you don't draw it to separate from people; you draw a line in the sand to separate from you. People then separate themselves from you for their own personal reasons, but that is none of your business.

It is okay to see something special in others, admire what you see, and be confident in others; in fact, you want to be around people who impart within you confidence, boldness, and the importance of having a strong sense of self. Many people don't know how to exist around winners because of what they refuse to see in themselves. Their negative disposition is not a reflection of what they are not capable of, it is a reflection of their inability to believe in themselves. We all know people like this, but more importantly, we know the factors that contribute to the negativity they cast onto others whether we choose to believe it is on us. Either way you have to be mindful of the negative influence you allow in your life, whether it is family, friends, associates, or strangers because negativity does not serve anyone, negativity serves negativity. If you allow negativity any space in your being, it won't stop spreading until it consumes you. You can't limit negativity you either embrace it or get rid of it, because it cannot coexist with the vision God has placed in your heart.

I did not consider the negativity that could come my way and did not acknowledge the negativity that did. What I believed people would think was very influential on why I was hiding in the first place so I was determined to not let what people thought stop me again. Not everyone will understand your passion, drive, and resiliency, which is why it takes courage to be yourself. You will have to continue through the ridicule, the laughs, the isolation, and the disbelief. When you take that first step into the unknown, you cannot passively believe you are one among many…you have to live as though you are (what/who you see yourself becoming without holding the title) and you are becoming (becoming greater than you imagined when you lacked courage).

What is Your Message | Marques Roberts

The Doctor, the Comedian, the Lawyer, the Teacher, the Plumber, and the Politician are all those things long before we meet them…they only lack the title. You must be whatever you are working toward right now; you are just at a different point in your journey than those who have received a title. Those years in the developmental leagues, the countless hours working as waiters, grocery baggers, Uber drivers, bartenders, residents and even exotic dancers during undergrad/graduate studies; the numerous no's and new lows from disappointments experienced in failed auditions/interviews are all a part of the process that many before you defined and many after you will redefine. The difference is there are people who only accept this is a part of their journey that helps build them and there are those who cannot see past the moment allowing the misfortune to dictate their path. The people who made it did not make it by stopping; they looked and felt just like you on their journey. Don't allow yourself to see the success you wish to obtain and be blind to the process. The title is the only thing given; the identity is discovered and evolves through the process.

Be courageous enough to decide that the title is yours and let nothing stop you from seeing it through. After you receive the title, don't stop; continue to become a better version of yourself in that role. Redefine and provide a new experience of what that role looks like for everyone aiming to follow in your footsteps. If your effort ever stops before or after you receive the title, it is then that you stop being. Whatever we are seeking is waiting for our time and effort to position us to receive it. We must have the courage to continue to make the investment to keep becoming and not accept someone else's lies or misfortune as our destiny. When we accept the lies or box ourselves in mentally, we unconsciously stop putting forth the effort because we rid ourselves of the belief and the courage it takes to beat the odds.

Most people who accept limits in their lives live in constant regret and bitterness. They have become accustomed to watching others live or they are consumed with pretending to be something they are not because they lack the courage to act on their ambition. When you begin to act in courage in the face of your obstacles, you draw from God's well of love that insists you are already victorious. If you can build a routine of living in courage, relationship pushes you from searching for victory to walking in victory, which frees you from the bondage of mental blocks. Instead of being distracted by your fears, your confidence leads you to be fully invested in all that you do. You embody the victory in your ups and downs, as your circumstances no longer have the power to dictate who you are. You dictate who you become based on God's promises creating your circumstances.

Long before any acknowledgment, appreciation, and awards, it is important to learn to witness your success and to cherish the value of the reward the process brings. Reward is part of the unseen that God has placed in all of us. As courage drives us through the obstacles to make the unseen come to pass, we realize the value of the external accomplishment is minimal in comparison to the internal reward. Relationship forces us to acknowledge His presence in our lives and what He has done in us through the process instead of focusing on a new standard, goal, or record we have achieved. Reward creates a new being within or a new identity, rewards pull us to a place of accountability we must acknowledge every time we begin to veer off in the wrong direction, reward is a glimpse into God's will for our lives. Once you have become familiar with exhibiting courage in the face of obstacles, relationship reinforces that you should not be afraid of what you don't know, but be afraid of the lies you once accepted as truth to avoid experiencing the pain of the undone.

Chapter 6

WILLINGNESS

Making Yourself Available and Giving Maximum Effort in All Opportunities to Experience God, Enabling Others to Experience God Through You

There is a void in the universe created by God's will for our lives that can only be tapped into by the individual the void was created for…You! When you decide to step into this void, what He has in store for you begins to seek you out because there is no longer a void where it was trying to go. Partnerships, network, information, resources, ideas, and opportunity all reveal themselves because you were willing to step out in faith and make yourself available. An empowering element of this principle is that all these things are tailored for you, so you don't have to focus on perfection or standards, you don't have to be guarded and hesitant; you must only be willing to be the best version of yourself to receive what is already waiting for you.

One definition of willing is "done." This is ironic because our victories, our story, our destiny, our achievements beyond our wildest dreams are done, but only in relation to our level of submission and obedience or, simply put, our willingness. We waste so much time on planning, organizing, or other basic forms of control that we overlook the invaluable impact of authenticity, freedom, and innocence in just doing. Society suggests that it takes specific qualifications, achievement, knowledge, money, and perfect timing before we should even try to pursue our dreams, but this mentality could not be further from reality. If we only act based on standards such as these we'd never do and not doing only leads to prolonged pain and misery. I don't have many regrets in life, but I do regret the times I didn't try at all or didn't try my best. I fall short weekly, but this always leads to improvement and/or success because failure is only failure when we allow it to be; things may not go how we want, but what we learn in the process of doing teaches us how to make the next attempt better if we are willing to own our role in falling short.

The journey of being the message is constant, which is significant because in the process of building the habit of willingness, we undo the thought patterns, routines, beliefs, and the lifestyle they create that leads us to relinquish our responsibility as His vessels. All of our routines must be examined because our perspective creates numerous blind spots when our thoughts don't acknowledge the value and power every person possesses. This does not mean we are responsible for knowing the impact we will have in every direct/indirect encounter, but we are responsible for being our best in the moment, especially when knowing impact is a possibility. It is not possible to know what every person you encounter is going through and you are not expected to know. However, this does not mean God will not use you. In fact, not knowing makes your impact that much more humbling for yourself and those you impacted because the experience reveals more of God's character to you. We simply cannot comprehend the endlessness and complexity of the impact we have on each other through simply being, which only makes our willingness that much more critical. When you live to serve with the right intent and experience God stepping in it doesn't take long to realize it was you that has always been in your way.

In most cases when we fail to make ourselves available or challenge ourselves to take our lives/careers to the next level, we are operating with a me-first attitude. When we are our priority everything else suffers. Selfish fear and foolish pride keep us from doing and causes us to remain in our comfort zone. A me-first attitude protects our pride with excuses and lies for why we don't give our best effort and keeps us safe from the unknown by limiting what we are open to experiencing. This enables us to exist while never pushing us to live. Turning away from the emptiness of doing just enough and being willing to submit to the process of progress by giving our best effort is a daily choice. Choosing to show up and choosing to give our best effort opens us up to have experiences versus being present to pass time. Being vulnerable and true to ourselves empowers us and others through witnessing how no gimmick, no strategy, no agenda, just the pure form of our passion, authenticity, all-out effort, and transparency connects, uplifts, and challenges those around us.

I like to break willingness down to two pillars, availability and effort, meaning always being open-minded or showing up and always giving our best. Our willingness carries us into God's will increasing our capacity to be used, as willingness is an extension of our faith. Only faith makes you show up in unlikely circumstances and put forth an effort that changes lives. When exposed to the spirit and influence of a willing vessel in action, there is an experience where many gain confidence and fervor through what they witness. In the same breath, others are humbled and redirected because their experience reveals their intent is self-serving. That is the power He has through us and in us when we are willing to submit. He is able to awaken us in Him by seeing glimpses of our greatness in the experiences of others. As what we witness builds us up, we are redirected as we analyze the value of the experience for ourselves and others versus what we did not get because we sought to serve ourselves.

Being willing is similar to the Yes Experiment, where people say yes to everything asked of them for 30 days. Saying yes opens their mind and provides experiences they previously would have never considered. People in the Yes Experiment often gain a new perspective that changes their willingness. For me, being willing to remain engaged and empowering myself instead of my opposition has pushed me to have more presence and even speak up in settings where I would normally have felt inadequate, awkward, and out of place. My progression is a direct result of being willing to do what needs to be done outside my comfort zone. I can attribute a portion of the progression to my willingness to join Toastmasters as a challenge to myself to change this area of my life. Toastmasters forced me into settings that promote conversing and engaging. Not only is it promoted, it is often used as a topic of discussion to establish commonality among members who struggle in this area. The classes provided an encouraging, sacred, and judgment-free zone for individuals to feel safe to grow. The more I engaged weekly, the more my anxiety decreased, the more roles I volunteered for, and the more my apprehension subsided each week. As I witnessed these mountains getting smaller in class, I saw the investment transfer into the workplace and my personal life as exchanges with strangers, coworkers, bosses, and other acquaintances went from being intimidating and awkward to familiar and refreshing.

Each time I get over myself to just be myself, I find it easier to do so going forward. What we can accomplish is truly amazing when we are willing to show up and submit to the process of change instead of ignoring the elephant in the room. Change requires deliberate all-out effort to create the difference we want to see. The bonus is we become accustomed to facing challenges or tackling giants in our lives, and the same willingness shows up in other areas when we begin to feel those familiar inklings of fear, inadequacy, and intimidation. This does not mean the work gets easier, but our perspective changes regarding how we view the process and what we now see in ourselves. When your perspective evolves, it is one of the most rewarding elements of your willingness. You begin to see your true value as you rewrite your truth by smashing stereotypes, erasing standards, and destroying limits you allowed to place your life in a chokehold.

There is Not a Bird Flying With Its Feet on the Ground

The idea of perfection is intimidating and regularly serves as a huge roadblock, preventing us from stepping out on faith. The truth is perfection does not exist until we create it. If we focus on status, standards, or any other external factors, we limit ourselves and, more importantly, we limit God in our lives. In sports, analysts say a pitch is a bad pitch until the batter hits it over the fence; the jump shot is a horrible choice until it goes through the net, or the pass is a bad decision by the quarterback until the referee signals a touchdown. The professional athletes the analysts are critiquing have not reached their level of success by limiting themselves to ideologies and theories, they are there because they were willing to believe when others shied away, work when others could not see the benefit, and act despite what the odds may have suggested. As people, the majority of us have been misled by the idea of perfection. In chasing perfection we disregard the value of doing as we focus on questioning our capability based on bias, stereotypes, culture, and standards, causing us to never believe in ourselves enough to do.

No matter what you choose to be, philanthropist, pastor, secretary, farmer, mechanic, teacher, doctor, athlete, or entertainer, you can be successful. Just don't become so overwhelmed with trying to be successful that you ground yourself in fear. The key with success is knowing the true definition of success is subjective and that every individual should have a personal definition of what success means to them. Many of us make the mistake of allowing someone else's definition of success to become our own. Our friends want something so we want it; our parents have their idea of what success is so they instill it in us. We watch the media give people the title of successful so we tell ourselves we should pursue what they accomplished. We all have the power to choose to be successful, the level of success we desire, and the freedom to work toward it but we create a huge problem for ourselves in failing to define what success means to us. When we don't have that personal definition we aim to be successful based on someone else's opinion. This is a scary place because without external validation you constantly label yourself unsuccessful. In defining success we take the power back that gave to opinions and deploy it in our work. In our willingness to work we find ourselves in a place of success because true success is achieved through acting. Take your power back by defining what success is in your life then be successful daily by refusing to succumb to the internal/external odds, opposition, and obstacles before you as you work towards your vision.

A willing person is a successful person because they are constantly bringing their vision to fruition. They seem to always be positive or on the move because they are doing instead of contemplating. Remember in each vessel "faith looks like something" so faith should be on display. Courage implies we are not to be deterred so we embrace opposition and with willingness it is done so we step out of that which we are to be that which we are becoming. Too many of us suffer from routines where we allow ourselves to embrace excuses whether it is settling, fear, pursuit of perfection or paralysis by analysis. We uncomfortably settle in a state of waiting where we comfortably avoid the discomfort of finding/making our way. True willingness is working through the discomfort as you boldly step out of your comfort zone in faith instead of passively ignoring the fact that you are not willing to believe in yourself in the unknown.

Most birds leave the nest prior to learning how to fly. They are comfortable in the nest, but they are willing to face the unknown because they know they were not created to sit. Their discomfort with being out of place outweighs the comfort of the nest so much they do whatever it takes to step into their purpose. The unknown fate of leaving the nest is not enough to stop the birds from going against all odds and becoming. The birds know God has done magnificent works in them, but they must first go through the process of facing the unknown outside of their comfort zone to experience God's work.

We must all spend time in the unknown or the dark at some point if we wish to grow, to progress, or to reach a specific level of success. The dark or the unknown equals isolation, where there is nothing but you and the work it takes to bring light back into your situation. Once you are in the dark, it is sink or swim. You can either quit so the ocean of the unknown can wash you up on the shores of your comfort zone or swim through the waves and storms until you break through the horizon to a new place of existence. When you break through, there isn't anyone or anything that can take away what you know you know. Everyone may not understand when you have come through the dark, but they can sense the calm in your demeanor, the peace in your spirit, the confidence in your quiet, and the precision in your presence because the dark has taught you how to navigate the light. The process of breaking through changes you; the identity you discover working through the dark of life outside the nest becomes embedded as the process teaches you how to trust yourself. The moment you learn to believe in yourself is like giving birth to a new you, and the new you changes your approach to life as the experience has taught you to feel His pull, to hear His voice, see the enemy at work, understand purpose, find peace in chaos, remain stable in silence, and embrace the power of being a wholly submitted vessel soaring through life outside the nest.

You Have to be Uncomfortable That You're Comfortable with Being Uncomfortable

A willing vessel is dangerous to barriers, to stereotypes, to dated divisive and restrictive tradition, to broken culture, to empty religion, and to unquestioned routine. If you are willing to do God's will (Be the message), you are considered dangerous to other people in your circumstances because there is no settling, there is no not asking why, there is no giving up on what you believe in, there is no submitting to circumstances, there is no accepting standards and no accepting people who are not willing. If they are prone to conforming, whether it's your family, coworkers, strangers, or friends they know they cannot confine you to the limits they have placed on themselves and others who allowed them to do so. Willing people aren't afraid of disruption. In fact, their willingness brings others face to face with their own insecurities because experiencing someone willing to pay the cost of obedience makes them realize they've settled because of their own fears that won't allow them to believe in themselves enough to survive their personal journey of obedience.

Long before a willing person speaks their spirit and disposition stir up the energy wherever they go. It is not a bad thing, but it is something you have to be aware of because you will come in contact with those who are unfamiliar with willing spirits who have a predisposition to resist because they perceive the disruptive essence of your being as negative. Assumed negativity pushes people to withdraw or put up a wall which makes it critical to know your role is not to win people over, your role is to plant and water seeds for an awakening in the spirit. If you're focusing on their disposition then you've lost direction in your approach because now you're prioritizing pleasing people versus being (Stay aligned with your assignment). This is a tough place because your being pushes you into a place of leadership so others place their discomfort on your plate whether they are following you or simply inspired by you. Be aware so you prioritize staying aligned and know what you are facing as there is a difference in how to handle discomfort and how to handle opposition.

When it is time to do (to take action), comfort is a casualty of disruption. The awakening you cause from your infectiousness pushes people to finally move and ask questions later. The when, who, and how take care of themselves when we are bold enough to do. Your being alone does work you cannot comprehend, so focusing on being about His will instead of how to win people over is critical to you not getting in your own way. Those who stand in opposition are victorious every time you allow them to push you to focus on you or them. Their fear and insecurity push them to go to any length to disrupt or disprove you. They try to make you forget who you are, use petty attacks to turn others against you, and even antagonize you until they steal your attention from your responsibility. While others, overwhelmed by the implications of change, move out of the way; knowing something greater is driving you that they cannot prevent.

What we have to understand is our power when we are willing and the magnitude of what it means to walk in it versus passively accepting things as they are. The same way a willing vessel won't allow others to get in their way, they won't allow themselves either. There is no place a willing vessel will not go, there is no empty routine they will not disrupt, there are no internal/external preferences that provoke prevention, and there are simply no circumstances to stop a willing vessel from stepping up and being available to be used.

When was the last time you embraced an opportunity outside your comfort zone? When was the last time you decided to release the reigns and let God have His way in your circumstances? If you are always in control, where does God have room to show up in your life? When you have no control, know that God has absolute control. You were brought to whatever challenges you are facing to be used. You must be willing to own the journey as an opportunity and not oppose the journey as a burden. When life brings us to instances where our willingness does not match up with the demands of our journey, we retreat to our comfort zones. A place where physically and mentally, life does not challenge us, people don't challenge us, and we are not held accountable to ask more of ourselves. We just go about each day ignoring the fact that we are unfulfilled ignoring our instincts and chasing distractions to avoid facing the reality that we have given up on the journey and ourselves. We don't have to be distracted when we know we are capable of more. So if you are chasing distractions, the first step of getting out of your own way is to stop running, because you cannot outrun yourself.

When I left Baylor University, I rushed back to Luling to be in my comfort zone, fearful of the next chapter of life and ashamed that I had nowhere else to go. I did not know what to do about my situation, and I felt I had nowhere to turn if it did not involve football. No place was more comfortable than among my closest friends, where we spent 70 to 80 percent of our time under the influence of drugs or alcohol. Here, not only was I not questioned, but I was also able to avoid myself. Day after day I chased distraction after distraction to avoid facing myself and the truth that I was capable of doing more. I was afraid of stepping into unfamiliar circumstances to learn how to do more. Because of my lack of willingness to get uncomfortable, I spent almost two years running from my truth until I got fed up with being uncomfortable with what I had become and where I was not headed. I wanted an opportunity, but I had not made that known to anyone. I had not submitted any resumes, and I never made myself available to anyone besides friends who would not question or challenge me.

That day when my mom told me I had to go, instead of continuing to run, I decided I had to get back in the game of life if I wanted to change my situation. I was uncomfortable at the thought of what it would take, but we must work through the discomfort of life's challenges instead of finding comfort in running, emptiness, or misery. I began by opening up to others about my desires, making it known that I wanted to leave Luling and do more with myself. This is when I asked my future wife if she knew of any opportunities in the Houston area. She sent me the information and within a month I was in Houston interviewing. About a month later, I was on a plane to Tennessee for training. I had not ever been transparent about my desires and I really had no clue of how to ask about job opportunities or complete a resume. Only a few conversations later and the required submission to the vulnerability of my situation enabled me to ask questions I was not accustomed to asking and receiving help I did not know I needed. This game of life is tough, but cutting ourselves off only lessens our experience. It is no longer okay to remain on the sidelines; we must get in the game and bring our best to this stage we call life to experience the true performance of God. If we are willing to participate, God will orchestrate.

I was so unfamiliar to the working world and so consumed with not losing my job in the midst of trying to survive I had no clue I had become a victim of complacency. I got so stuck in a routine of getting by, I allowed myself once again to limit my exposure to experiences and people who possessed the insight to make me question the path of my life. I settled in college when I was not confident enough to step up. I settled at home after college because I was not willing to get uncomfortable. Those experiences taught me I could not point my finger anywhere except at myself because it was what I was not doing that led to my circumstances. The pain I felt from being stuck once again taught me if you don't change on the inside, it does not matter where you go, you will just be the same person in a new place. From that point forward, I vowed to never let myself grow roots again or look to blend in when I knew God had taught me through years of isolation that I had to step up and be bold.

In your life, it could be your health, your career, or even a relationship. Whatever the situation is, make sure that you have not adapted to circumstances you know you should not be in. We buy new clothes when we gain weight instead of changing our diets and exercise routines. We complain about our role at our job, but we never take ownership of the fact that we are not adding value to our employer or ourselves through extra effort. We limit ourselves to completing the tasks asked of us and seek to stay under the radar instead of being the willing vessel that disrupts the workplace culture and/or changes our professional trajectory. In relationships, we allow ourselves to be mistreated or disrespected then make excuses for that person's actions or even demean ourselves to avoid dealing with the truth. Some of us are simply too prideful to admit we need work so we subscribe to the lies we feed ourselves and turn a blind eye to the work we are not willing to submit to. Whatever your situation, you cannot continue to ignore or lie to yourself about the fact that you are not fighting for the life that is waiting for you. Where have you created a blind spot for foolish pride in your life? In what area have you become complacent with your lack of effort? Where do you consistently make excuses for accepting less than instead of demanding more? Where you want more, you must first demand it from yourself, where you were once intimidated to go, you have to show up, wherever you allowed "me" to say no, "you" have to be willing to say yes. Be uncomfortable with less than and make it a point to accept the challenge from yourself to do the work required until you can be pleased knowing you are giving your best effort.

Opportunity Is Constant; You're Just Not in Position

I stated earlier that an Executive said to me, "Shit, you create your own opportunities." In opposition to that statement, many people point out that there is a lack of opportunity. I understand the thought process or sentiment behind creating your own opportunity, but I don't think we literally create opportunity, and I know there is not a lack thereof. Relationship has taught me that opportunity is constant, we just seize moments when we are in position. Our problem is, in most cases, we have no perspective or we have a second-hand perspective that prevents us from getting into position or even being aware of opportunity. In other words, a lack of His presence means a lack of perspective, resulting in us being influenced by personal preference. When we reach a place where we are so enamored or caught up in what we want, what we need, and how things should look that we never move we have turned preference into prevention. In these cases, you have to really examine the purpose the preference is serving. Ninety-nine percent of the time, preference flows from selfish pride or selfish fear. They limit your vision, preventing you from doing what you should do based on what you want or what you feel is safe. Safety is never guaranteed and doing is the only way you truly learn how to. In prideful and fearful preference, we don't search for how to, we search for why not. You can always find a why not, and in many cases, your *why not* is tied to God's *why*. The next time you find a *why not* remember God's *why* or your 'how to' is on the other side of you doing.

If we invest time and effort when we don't know what is in front of us, we gain more opportunities because we develop a greater awareness and appreciation for opportunity that helps us seize it in areas where we previously were resistant or completely failed to recognize what was in front of us. If our focus is on effort, growth, and availability, we have no time to focus on "what's not" because the reward of the investment will not allow us to miss seizing "what is." "What's not" causes us to go through the motions instead of selling out because what we don't see pushes us to protect our pride. When we go through the motions, we miss the opportunity as a vessel to experience God where we have nothing left to give and we miss the opportunity to impact others with the God in us.

When we lack effort we fail to get in position and when we lack passion we do not provide the energy that others connect to. You see, maximum effort brings us to a place where we have no more, and when we are willing to go there, we witness God pick up where we had no more to give. This does not only apply to an athlete in the "zone." It means as a parent, a spouse, an employee, or any other walk in life; when we sell out, God goes all in. Stop holding back to protect your pride and make yourself vulnerable, because the pain that life causes can't surpass the peace that God provides. As long as you feel safe in your effort, you will feel unfulfilled or shortchanged in your experience because you will only focus on "what's not." But when you are willing to let go and be vulnerable, you make the most of "what is." And where you would normally assume there was a shortage in you or your situation, God picks up and surpasses anything you could conceive.

In the fall of 2014, a friend who is a motivational speaker said to me, "You know my tour is coming to Houston; I want you to come out." I replied, "Man, you know I know…I'm already there." Then he said, "No, I want you to speak." I said, "What! Man, naw. That's you, that ain't me." He then replied, "No, for real, I want you to speak." I continued to try and talk my way out of it, but after a little more back and forth I said, "Alright I got you, I'll do it." I never intended to do any public speaking, so I was really caught off guard and lost about what to do. In an attempt to be proactive, I let another friend know I was interested in encouraging others. About a month later, she called and asked, "Hey, you said you wanted to start speaking, right? Well in a few weeks, I'm singing at this church that is about an hour and half drive from you and you are scheduled to speak as well." I was caught off-guard, I was nervous, I felt completely out of my element and overwhelmed, I could even feel myself trying to find a way to get out of it, but instead of running I said, "Okay, I'll be there. Thank you!" I spent those next couple of weeks preparing to the best of my ability instead of wasting my time trying to find an excuse. Over the next few months, I kept being available and spoke anytime I got an opportunity. During this time, I learned that not only did I like speaking, but I am extremely passionate about encouraging people. My friend's event had approximately 500 people in attendance and the time I invested leading up to the event provided me the experience I needed to be confident enough in myself to deliver.

Prior to the event, I invested my time to become comfortable presenting, but afterward, I invested my time to become a better speaker. I began to study speakers by listening to them during my daily commute to work and back home. I also made my car my practice facility because my family occupied my time when I got home and I did not want to wake them up by practicing after they went to sleep. In the beginning, I accepted everything thrown at me, and I failed miserably on multiple occasions. But I did not allow these experiences to steal my willingness to be available and give my best. Over time, my efforts paid off, as my lowest moment in speaking helped me establish the foundation for who I am as a speaker.

I was invited to speak at a Martin Luther King Jr. program in Victoria, Texas. Because of my inexperience, I made many incorrect assumptions. I prepared for weeks for what I thought would be an auditorium where I would be the sole form of entertainment and have everyone's attention. Instead of the stage being a focal point for the attendees, it was more like a platform for background noise. To set the scene, the event center, circular in shape, had vendors around 60% of the wall beginning from the side entrance all the way around the back half of the Coliseum. Each vendor had exhibits/booths set up where they were providing information, selling merchandise, or selling food. In the center area of the back half of the room, rows of tables were set up for dining. Twenty to thirty feet opposite the area designated for eating were chairs set up for attendees who wanted to enjoy the provided entertainment in the front half of the room.

I watched a couple of groups and individuals give their presentations and be completely ignored before it was time for my presentation. When I walked onto the stage, I realized it was 3–4 feet off the ground and there was a space that was about 20 feet from the first row of the audience that was be used as a play area for the kids in attendance. As I spoke, the noise from the event drowned me out. On top of that, my inexperience with this type of setting did not give me the confidence I needed to adapt and make the most of the presentation.

I learned several valuable lessons about preparation, communication with organizers, presentation presence, and navigating the location. The most important lesson I learned was staying in my lane where I was an expert on the subject matter of my speeches. My mom and my wife tried blaming the event hosts for the terrible organization. A few people in the audience came up to acknowledge the value of my content and extended an invitation for future events, but I could not get over the fact that I was overwhelmed and had no command.

During the ride home, my wife tried telling me I did well, but I would not hear it. Then she made a suggestion that would alter my life, "You know, you should stick to your message." She was referring to my speeches and tailoring my presentation from event to event. This led me to ask myself, "What is your message." It would become the guiding principle for my life at work, with my family, in every speech to come, in my eating/exercising, in this book, and in my complete existence.

Through my trials, I found my voice, defined my intent, and understood who I am as a speaker, not who I felt audiences wanted me to be. As I gained confidence in speaking, I gained the same confidence in the workplace and understood my significance in all walks of life was valuable. It became clear that my ultimate contribution, my message, comes from my willingness to be true to myself. The more I made myself available, the more I found myself succeeding outside of my comfort zone. I was in position, so opportunity was finding me. In every instance, at work or a new speaking engagement, I gave my all and grew despite the outcome and in any instance where I held back, because I lacked of confidence, I ended up sulking in regret as I was hurt by the lackluster product I allowed to be a representation of myself.

In 2015 I was tapped to be the Lead for my employer's Organizational Change Management (OCM) program that covers 25,000 employees. My responsibilities required doing presentations at each facility in front of staff, management, and executive leadership. I would have never accepted this responsibility in the past, but when I am presented with an opportunity now, I think about the pain I experienced when I had no other options and went back home so sit on the corner after college because I was not willing to invest in myself outside of my comfort zone. After a year of leading this program, I was asked to present our OCM story at the Cerner Health Conference. This conference hosts over 14,000 Healthcare professionals and officials from around the country over 6 or 7 days. Our presentation would be one of the largest partner presentations on Monday morning in front of approximately 600

Healthcare Professionals from across the country. I immediately became excited about the opportunity and began to thank God for the past 3 years of work. I knew in my heart that without Toastmasters and volunteering at churches, schools, non-profits, recovery, and intervention programs, I would not have had the confidence to move forward.

When I began preparing, the first question I asked myself was, "How do I make this me?" I reviewed the content I was to deliver, and then revisited my experiences at the facilities I'd visited over the past year. I came up with a presentation I felt good about delivering, not the presentation I thought the attendees wanted to hear. This is another reason it is critical that you are willing to be available, willing to be your best, and willing to be true to yourself because this is how you develop the confidence to trust yourself to execute. In the most opportune and critical moment of my professional career, I had the confidence and wherewithal to take ownership of my contribution and not conform to outside influences or any internal noise. I knew the only way I would be successful was to own the presentation and bring myself to it. Willingness not only helps you become comfortable with who you are, it empowers you to be comfortable with whom you are not. Our peers rated the presentation the highest of all partners and clients who presented throughout the week. Even weeks after the presentation, I received compliments from Cerner employees and other partners.

Who I have become is far from who I was, and who I am becoming is far from who I am now, but that does not diminish my value as a person at any stage of life. God has, does, and will use you as you are. He knows your value right where you stand and you should too. When I look back, I have more understanding of my value at each stage of my life and I also see how my perception of myself diminished that value. If I'd seen then what I see now, I would have had set a different level of expectations and standards for myself.

What we see is affected by what we know. We must change our narrative by changing our willingness to obtain information and experience. To gain a more Godly perspective, we must be willing to go get our own information and live our own experiences instead of accepting what is passed to us as truth. If we live based on second-hand experience and information, we will never see the constant opportunity God has placed in in our lives, because we have no perspective. The insight encountered in personal experience and knowledge gained from gathering information changes our perspective. Experience empowers us because the time we invest brings about familiarization and reassures us of His presence. The confidence gained in familiarity implores us to step up, to speak up, and to get up when we fail. In speaking up, stepping up, and getting up, we soon find ourselves in unfamiliar circumstances more often because where we once saw nothing, we now see opportunity. The ability to consistently see opportunity is evidence of changed or newfound perspective. When our perspective changes, perceived facts turn into opinions and our minds are freed to envision countless possibilities through recognizing infinite opportunity.

Chapter 7

CONSISTENCY

Responding to the Challenges of Each Day by Keeping Your Principles Intact in Thought, Speech, and Action

One of the biggest mistakes we make is trying to discipline our consistency when consistency is proven to be a disciplinarian. I can't count how many Mondays that have served as the start of a "new lifestyle" for me. When seeking change or progression it's natural for us to search for emotions, standards, or other factors i.e. timelines or settings from our past that we associate with the discipline that drove us to achieve past goals. In revisiting our 'glory' days we acknowledge the standard, but fail to understand that we're trying to recreate discipline that we have to rebuild. And the only way to rebuild that discipline is through consistency. As we move through life it is advantageous for us to be able to draw from past experiences, but we can handicap ourselves by seeking to duplicate the experiences versus gleaning from them. Success in the present requires a new investment and a new discipline that we all have to discover. The greatest challenges of the process, when trying to progress, are starting journey and remaining consistent through completion. The majority of successful entrepreneurs echo the same sentiment "get started". What this means is, stop focusing on things that don't matter (Could've, should've, would've) and take action so you have a starting place to build from. Otherwise you'll find yourself always working towards a place to start instead of building and producing. Starting is important as the experience serves as our initial sample/product of our effort and execution informing us of the effort required to build and execution required to continue producing. After starting it is our consistency that creates the growth and progression that not only serves as reward, but also incentive to keep going as we become accustom to conquering the unknown.

Consistency undresses us layer by layer, pushing us to acknowledge our shortcomings and successes along with our weaknesses and strengths while demanding that we let nothing stop us from asking for more from ourselves. In fact, consistency teaches us we have to continue to give more, but it is our responsibility to learn what more is in our lives. After being stripped down by consistency the easiest thing to do is give up on yourself by focusing on all that you aren't. When you focus on all that you aren't, you lessen all that you are. As you reduce your being you are left with a poor attitude that is void of peace that fosters poor effort to protect your pride. You do things like give half-hearted effort so you can say "I didn't even try my best" or you don't even bother to show up in most cases to sell yourself on the lie that you don't care. Sometimes it's just the pressure of knowing challenges are coming so you refuse to submit to avoid disappointment down the line. In protecting our pride the only thing we're consistent at is being inconsistent. When we don't believe in our effort we subconsciously don't expect anyone else to believe in us, therefore, we never produce anything because without faith in who we are we refuse to execute.

When I first heard an Eric Thomas speech on YouTube, over 10 years ago, I immediately connected to his passion. Years later, when I began to study speakers, it was passion I connected to as I first heard Les Brown, Zig Ziglar, and Jim Rhome. My attraction did not register to me until people began to let me know it was my passion that touched them when they heard me speak. As I received praise for my presentations I also received criticism. Instead of using that criticism for fuel, I allowed it to redirect my energy. As a result, instead of "doubling/tripling down" on my strengths, as Gary Vee (Vaynerchuk) would say, I focused all my energy on my weaknesses. I began working to be all that I wasn't to please critics versus owning all that I was to serve people. While my effort helped me to grow in some areas, my thinking disregarded my significance and placed a ceiling on my abilities. It took a few years, before I finally stopped dwelling on all that I wasn't and turned my energy towards how to best deploy what makes me significant. Changing my thoughts and redirecting my energy has led to more execution and production which is very exciting and motivating. Still, I have to fight myself to be consistent in not letting my old ways creep back in and rob me of my peace, direction, confidence, determination and vision because consistency/inconsistency begins in our spirit and our thoughts before it shows up in our actions.

Even When You Aren't, You Are Intentional

Consistency reveals truth that humbles us, progression that motivates us, mental capacity that empowers us, experience that reassures us, glimpses of greatness that challenges us, and relationship that embraces us at every turn on God's path for our lives. In the same breath, consistency also reveals habits, beliefs, emotions, and behaviors that stifle us and prevent us from continuing in God's will. Consistency provides truth that we have to face and own in totality if we wish to build the discipline required to maximize our potential. If we are not willing to take ownership of the truth consistency provides we are forced to bear the burden of our inconsistency.

In working to be consistent we bear the burden of becoming through the deliberate effort to separate ourselves from where we are. Separating becomes a priority because when you work from a place of truth you see all that you are and all that you aren't. In turn, the same truth pushes you to work tirelessly because you know you can and you will become. Believing in who we are and knowing we are headed somewhere are difference makers because sustaining our effort to create discipline not only requires consistent physical investment, but also consistent mental and spiritual investment. The physical shortcomings we witness through our inconsistent effort are the byproduct of a wavering mental and/or spiritual state. Faith says see all that you are, not all that you aren't. If we only see what we aren't we fail to be consistent because our effort is based on permission instead of approving of ourselves to be great. Not believing in ourselves, not knowing where we're headed, and not being intentional shows up as blameless immaturity, low self-esteem, deafening complacency, foolish arrogance, and restless impatience; all reflecting the state of our mental and spiritual inconsistency.

When we consistently give minimal effort or settle for doing just enough to get by consistency reminds us we are cheating ourselves of growth, revelation, progression, and relationship through receiving God's light in our lives or shedding His light in the lives of others. Again, we find ourselves in a place where we see why relationship is extremely important as it reinforces how our consistency serves a greater purpose. A life changing truth is that relationship aides you in understanding your identity. When you choose to not be consistent, relationship reminds you of your principles and values that are the pillars of your identity. Without consistency we fail to create relationship with Christ and those pillars have no foundation to support you as a person. When you have no foundation to stand on you stand on whatever protects your pride and hides your truth. This is a dangerous place because your truth is seen as a weakness pushing you into a routine of standing on lies to preserve yourself. In relationship we know Jesus has already preserved us, so our responsibility is to turn to Him to learn the power of His truth in order to learn to stand strong in our own truth. When discipline creates this foundation we have the support needed to wrestle against ourselves and our emotions to remain consistent as we build our lives.

Life moves at a very fast pace, so if you are not intentional with your time, emotions knock you off our path or throw you overboard, enabling life to toss you around like you are stranded in the sea. When stranded in a body of water, panicking is the first mistake you can make because the emotionally charged reaction of panicking causes you to exert the energy needed to survive. In life, we often make the same mistake as we allow emotions to rule our thoughts when we take on new responsibilities, face new beginnings, stare down adversity, encounter delay, or navigate any circumstances that make us uncomfortable. In these instances we react by being intimidated by our situations, then we become overwhelmed with stress/anxiety or we completely avoid the stress by shutting down (mentally) without giving ourselves a chance.

In moments of discomfort, it's the consistency in how we think that moves us past panicking to stabilizing ourselves enough to process information and assess our circumstances with clear thoughts. Keeping our principles intact begins with our thoughts then trickles down to our speech and actions. When our minds are clear, elements and emotions become secondary to purpose. Far too often we accept defeat or become a shell of ourselves based on the odds we perceive, when we should allow purpose to dictate our response to our circumstances. Consistently controlling our thoughts shows up in our behavior moving us from accepting to dictating. We go from being a shell of ourselves to stepping out of our shell to possess what is rightfully ours. As time progresses we recognize a difference in our approach, attempts, and production making us more aware of our propensity to get in our own way. Our awareness helps us to identify habits and routines related to us giving up control to our emotions because in becoming we grow to despise the helplessness we embodied that led to numerous circumstances we could have prevented.

In life, we have a vast audience that we impact daily with how we deal with challenges. Therefore, consistency is not simply a characteristic of your personality; it is a responsibility of your being. This is why true consistency is demanded in all areas of our life because inconsistency is just as influential as it is passed on in our thoughts, our words, and our actions. In most cases we pass inconsistency on unintentionally, never aware that what we exhibited was our signature of approval. Either your consistency or your inconsistencies tell your story, and you have the moment-to-moment, day-to-day power/responsibility of choosing which one tells yours.

From the time we are able to interpret behavior, we develop unconscious routines based on who and what we see and how what we see makes us feel. These routines begin empty of thought as the message of a "this is how it is" mentality is passed down. As time goes on, the same routines become the framework of our personalities and belief systems. We find ourselves operating based on the culture or unwritten rules of the environment we live in. If no one in your family has done it, then you can't; if your dad is not at home, you don't have a future; women are not capable of being as successful as men; I did not experience happily married parents growing up, so I cannot be happily married; if you cannot play sports, you have to sell drugs; if you are not white, then you are inferior; or even believing the traditional route of education is the only way to be successful.

These unconscious thoughts/beliefs and others similar to them cause us to live within the confines of the limits they imply and place those same limits on the people we encounter. We're required to pull ourselves out of this vicious cycle of manifesting these thoughts/beliefs in our lives, the lives of others, and passing them down generation to generation. If you are honest, can you identify how you've created routines of consistently not striving for excellence through welcoming limits into your life? Understanding how we operate based on what we've been exposed to, we have to learn the habits we've adopted. If we aren't willing to acknowledge our habits we'll never own the responsibility of asking for more from ourselves when emotions push us to turn to what's comfortable. We simply allow the inconsistency of our emotional state to control us through habits we adopted in our sea of circumstances.

When you begin your day, you are never 100% sure of what challenges you will face, but you cannot live life like you are panicking in the middle of the ocean, losing more control with each wave life throws at you. Contrary to what many of us grew up learning, we have the power, and it is up to us to pass on a new message by making conscious decisions about the opportunities, obstacles, and impact, before us. The ability to control how we think does not mean we have the power to rid ourselves of emotion. But it is important to God that we use the power he has given us to consider the source behind our choices and learn how many of our decisions are products of learned unconscious routine reactions versus consistent calculated responses.

The Difference Between Where You Are and Where You Want to Be Is What You Don't Want to Do

When we discuss trust, normally, the focus is on the ways others have violated our trust and the damage that the violation caused. Whether it is something someone said, didn't say, did, or didn't do; the experience of being exposed or vulnerable and being mishandled pushes you to avoid vulnerability or refuse to be exposed going forward. I bet, like me, just hearing about trust being violated takes your thoughts to instances or person(s) who caused you to distrust them. For some it was a chain of events and for others it was one dramatic event that removed that sense of safety and freedom that you held. What was that moment like for you, when your trust was broken? The moment when you felt like opening up was the biggest mistake you made to date. As you reflect on that moment I need you to remove others and the emotions you associate with those moments from your thoughts and focus on yourself. Because bigger than any pain they caused is the loss of trust you have for yourself that you allow to hold you captive in the safety of the trust-free zone you've created. Whatever hurt someone caused you is a reflection of them; don't let their actions change how you see you. External factors only have so much impact, but control is something they must receive from you.

Think about how much of you is not flourishing because of you being in your own way. At some point your inability to trust yourself to win at life began to have more influence on your decision making than your faith in yourself. Broken trust is an issue, but you have to change the focus from others to yourself with this issue to reestablish you believing in yourself to be better than your circumstances.

Have you ever considered your lack of trust for yourself that prevents you from being the person you are capable of being? How often do you first consider the obstacles when a challenge is proposed versus considering your ability to be successful? Think about your choices and how you routinely choose what allows you to remain complacent versus what challenges you. One of my first challenges as a speaker was embracing my truth. The second was learning to trust myself. I didn't want anything to do with either initially because of my fear of being inadequate.

I just knew the audience would laugh this country boy off the stage because I was not eloquent enough. In public speaking it is normal to question yourself. The source of half of your feelings is the honor you have for the role and the source for the other half is fear. Every time I prepare a speech I have to stop myself from going down the path of figuring out what the audience wants to hear. I have to stop myself because trying to be something other than myself is a sign of lack of trust. Instead I do the exact opposite which is fully trust myself by giving the audience a piece of me. This used to be a struggle, because I had to learn to know I alone am enough. My feelings of inadequacy made me feel like I had to go outside of me. I would research stories that helped support my points, but were of no real interest to me. Ultimately this led to me being uncomfortable with my presentations because I was not comfortable with the content. If you don't know, when you are uncomfortable with your content or your responsibility it makes you nervous because you focus on everything that could go wrong versus focusing on execution. In sports the last thing you want is to get caught thinking because when you have to stop to think you are always catching up to those who are executing without stopping to think.

Lack of trust for ourselves pushes us to guess versus go. Guessing creates an inconsistency in our being because the randomness we embody in trying to gain control or convince ourselves we are in control. Ironically, true trust in ourselves is shown in our ability to let go and let God. Here, through faith, trust provides a consistency in our being that serves as a message to ourselves that empowers us to quit guessing and go.

After walking away from several events frustrated about my subpar speeches. I knew it was because my connection to the speech was not there and my only other option was to learn to trust myself. It wasn't what I wanted to do, but I knew it was what I had to do. When I give my story I am able to give more passion and dive into my truth. I am able to focus on leaving everything on the stage versus remembering facts. The problem was I didn't think I was enough so I was not willing to trust myself or my story. This led to off-the-wall presentations that had nothing to do with what I was about. My performances had no consistency and the roller-coaster of emotions I experienced during my speeches took so much out of me I was unable to receive from the experience. I knew what my specialty was, I knew what content I felt comfortable presenting, and I knew I had been afraid to let go. To this day the fear of trusting myself tries to creep back in. The difference now is I know where I want to be and I'm not letting anything, even myself, get in my way. It took me awhile to understand and accept I had to learn to trust who I am in Him versus trying to create a caricature of myself for people to love. Where is your level of trust for who you are in Him? Have you experienced that being or are you focused on build the caricature of yourself for others. Trusting you allows God to do work in you and through you. Learning to bet on myself, empowered me it allows us to build the trust we have for ourselves with each opportunity.

When we deliberately seek to be the message, purpose pushes us to give our best to life by reminding us God provides all we need to do His will. Instead we seek to be seen or we seek praise. In prioritizing ourselves, circumstances outweigh purpose in our decision-making. Whether it is our selfishness, fear, or lack of faith, we turn away from doing what we should to do what we perceive as more favorable. We find ourselves consistently taking the path that is the least challenging or not likely to get us out of our comfort zone. Somehow, in these moments, we make a routine of disassociating our dreams/goals from our routines or actions that define who we are. Our excuses, such as, tomorrow, next time, too many unfamiliar faces, need more people, only a few things in place, need more preparation, not enough money, or whatever story we choose is always enough not to act. If we want to achieve our goals we have to hold ourselves responsible for executing because what we don't do defines us just as much as what we do. No one has met the lazy, inconsistent, unpassionate, self-serving, non-present, and inactive person who was cherished for the impact they did not make based on all that they did not do.

It is in our own best interest to act now; begin building our foundation exactly where we are because it is the foundation, consisting of our core values and beliefs, which support/fuel the routine/progress we develop/experience and reapply/recreate to continue our success throughout life's journey. No one starts out wanting to sacrifice sleep or willingly subject themselves to ridicule. No one wants to give up their personal life to invest time in an idea that has no guaranteed return. No one wants to keep believing when they have been laughed at or felt like a failure because they were not able to deliver, not everyone is willing to pass up immediate return for long-term gain, but these struggles are a part of the process of fulfilling God's will. There is no secret to building your foundation; it's simply the willingness to stay true to you without compromising because it's the simple values we embrace early on that create separation from our circumstances, ourselves, and our peers that we must continue to embody as we move forward.

Consistently getting back up, believing you have what it takes, and pressing forward is the only way you shift your life from going through the process to growing through the process. The process assists in establishing our foundation by teaching us how to believe in ourselves to win the fight through taking punches, blocking punches, dodging punches, saving punches, and throwing our own punches back until we learn how to win. Through the commitment and discipline of our thoughts, energy, desires, and actions to win the external battles, we also learn the pillars of consistency it takes to win the internal war. With a solid foundation, you witness a difference in the consistency of your being in waking up knowing you have to fight, showing up to the fight, and giving your all each day regardless of the outcome rather than fearing the fight, passively avoiding the fight, and ultimately quitting because you're unwilling to lose the fight.

As much as hard work takes a toll on you physically, fighting is not possible without the mental capacity to push through. It takes a consistent, convinced, determined, and resilient mentality to live the vision versus allowing your dreams to remain thoughts that you never act upon. Consistent people look like where they are headed long before they reach their destination. It takes embodying the character, the principles, and the resiliency right where you are and then consistently deploying them to seize your vision daily when others are not willing to make the commitment. The people you admire and look to for inspiration consistently show up willing to submit to the process to do all they can to accomplish their goals and continue to live their dreams. What process are you unwilling to submit to? What is preventing you from embracing the pain or the hardships of growing? You cannot cut corners or wait it out, because cutting corners stunts your growth and waiting stops you from doing the work that changes you.

While I was training to run a 10K in 2015, the weather was very random, which is the norm for Texas winters. One day, while at work, the temperature dropped from 75+ degrees to the low 40's. When I was walking out to the parking lot, I thought "Wow, it's too cold to run today; I guess I'll have to wait until it warms up." This was my subconscious reaction with no hesitation, because I was not submitted to purpose. The unfavorable circumstances dictated my reaction despite knowing I had to stick to a strict running schedule to reach the goal I had set. I knew I was not ready to run the race, but I did not want to run in the cold. Circumstances defeated me with no resistance on my side at all. As I drove into my neighborhood, over an hour later and a couple degrees cooler, I saw the "usuals" out exercising and I said to myself, "Man, they're still getting it." I was intrigued by their level of consistency and in the same moment, I was also disciplined by consistency by being reminded of my lack thereof. When I thought about my health, my commitment, and the opportunity to inspire, my purpose began to outweigh my circumstances. Since I don't like to be chastised, I walked into the house, threw on some extra layers, and commenced to running. Running in the cold is not what I wanted to do, but it is what I had to do to get where I wanted to be.

Simple moments, like me walking out in the parking lot, are where we often embrace unconscious routines or toxic culture instead of enforcing ownership. What we see as minor often has a major impact, even something as simple as the snooze button. One day my wife once pointed out that I rushed the kids in the morning and it wasn't fair to them. Immediately that made me think, "Why am I rushing them" and my conclusion was the Snooze button. As I thought more about it I realized when I was hit the snooze button instead of getting up it causes me to run late, rush the kids, and be short-tempered with them because I'm stressed with getting them to school on time and making it to work on time. The mornings should be time we engage with our children and others. These are opportunities to love, enjoy, uplift, diffuse, or enlighten, but adding the stress of running late in any instance leads to us being less engaging, easily agitated, and/or appearing unapproachable. These moments for us to be springboards to a positive day or bright spots to a bad day become missed opportunities because of our lack of consistency. Another example is our effort in the gym. Showing up and putting your best into every rep of every set encourages you through the results and the light of your being encourages others to do the same. Witnessing your effort, consistency, and results motivates others to ask more of themselves instead of allowing themselves to feel defeated. At the same time, going through the motions and finding excuses for the results you are not getting is just as infectious as working hard and getting results. Going through the motions demonstrates to those who may be watching that it is okay to give less than your best as long as you prioritize excuses over results.

As a freshman the seniors at Baylor would say "Shiiii, I ain't lifting nothing" and walk out of the weight room during the season. Their influence led us to have a negative outlook toward the workouts and despise having to go to the gym because we thought it was a waste of time. After a couple of seasons it didn't take long to realize the importance of the weight room after experiencing how much stronger and faster the guys on the other teams were. On the other hand, when my wife began her journey of changing her lifestyle, supporting her led me to be inspired by her. I can remember looking at her workouts and saying to her "What! Ain't nobody doing all those reps". She said, "I know right, he's crazy" referring to her trainer. Even still day after day she kept going back and I stopped hearing about the reps and started seeing more determination in her being. As time passed I noticed her consistency was paying off as her body began to change. When she began to close in on competing in her first fitness competition I began to join her in her workouts for support and encouragement. As we went through these workouts I saw her go at it with no hesitation in regards to the exercise or the reps. I only saw her trying to get the most out of her investment. In that same week I found myself approaching the workouts and going through them with an intensity I hadn't had in almost 10 years. Witnessing her commitment and determination made me reach deeper and be more consistent about the time I committed. Ultimately, the seed she planted by going all in on her goals led me to setting a goal which resulted in me losing 35 pounds in 30 days. Not to mention she won three 1st place trophies and 1 2nd place trophy in her first competition!

Our level of awareness must be in tune at all times because habits and behaviors are so deeply embedded that the most uncritical moments act as gateways until we can establish new discipline. Think about routines that negatively impact where you are headed, but you unconsciously partake out of habit. Cool weather, warm weather, happy hour, the weekend, Friday afternoon/evening, kids going to bed, Saturday morning, Sunday afternoon, or playing golf with buddies. These are all windows of time or settings that trigger routines we have fallen into over the years that we use as an excuse to do what we want to do and turn away from what we don't want to do. There is nothing wrong with the routines if you are happy and at peace with your life, but if you want more, you have to do more. You have to set standards for yourself that say "as long as (whatever goal or desire) is not a part of my lifestyle then I have not afforded myself the luxury of this routine". Dedicating the time you previously gave to that routine to work towards where/what you want gives you time back for you. Along with that, your honor for your investment and progress pushes you to reevaluate if that routine is a harmless hobby or a lifeless anchor that you should cut ties with.

In assessing your time and investment you stand in a place of truth where you see the difference between the life you are living and the life you are seeking. What you don't want to do, is not all about the physical work of building; it includes the mental work of eliminating the routines/culture that prevent you from getting the work done to get to where God wants you to be. When we make up our mind to pursue a goal, we must establish a plan and then take ownership in executing it daily. When I did not execute in the process of losing the 35 pounds, it was not my circumstances or my ability that impacted how I went about my days. I could've easily accepted a lie as an excuse to not be consistent, but the truth is it was my fear of committing and coming up short that suggested I accept not giving my best. Then one day, frustrated that I was leaning towards giving up, I said to myself, "I already won." I decided that moment I already won because in fighting to become I defeated the norms I created. From that day forward, I committed to that consistent thought which elicited winning behavior instead of allowing fear to push me to embrace losing behavior to protect my pride. Facing our truth is tough, but we cannot be in God's will living from a place of fear. When I realized what was stopping me in the competition, I had to ask myself if the same fears were holding me back in life. In asking I already knew the answer, because if they weren't holding me back I would not have to ask. Now it's time to ask yourself, what is holding you back. What personal norms and routines have you established that you allow to control your thoughts and actions and why? The culture that you have created for how you lead your life is your downfall. If you won't accept that truth and you're refusing ownership, just know your inconsistency says otherwise.

Chasing More Makes Us Miss Gaining the Most

At times society and other external influences, in addition to arrogance, create a sense of entitlement. Time sacrificed, special treatment, loyal commitment, and pressure to succeed make us attach ourselves to projects, people, and causes, but that is part of the process we submit ourselves to, not validation for acknowledgment or compensation. We must remember regardless of the positive impact we intend to have on others; we are rewarded in being fulfilled. Because of external influences, it is important to have your HeadDownPushing, so the focus is consistently on God's will not approval or acknowledgment. While it may not be what you want to do, in seeking what He has in store instead of compensation or validation, gratitude meets you where you are and molds you as you move closer to not where you want to be, but where He wants you to be.

When you lack gratitude, you become inconsistent in intent by seeking honor or award from sources that can only underpay you for your contribution. If you did not start out looking for approval, don't lose yourself chasing it. There is no way to earn anything that cannot be paid for. Trust, confidence, passion, love, admiration, reward, wisdom, instinct, and influence are a few examples of what we cannot earn. They are all given and received by submitting yourself to the work before you—whether it is work on yourself, on your job, on a relationship, working out etc.

Faith should always reinforce expectation, but it should never make you arrogant enough to feel you deserve what cannot be measured nor defined. Often when we feel we deserve something, we are seeking validation, confirmation, or recognition from sources that could never truly repay us for the true value of our investment and impact. You cannot control how people see you, but you can control the consistency of your effort and intent to add value to the lives of others. Impact cannot be valued, measured, diminished, or denied, but it can be lost if we allow ourselves to lose consistency in our effort and intentions by acting selfishly on our own behalf.

My pro-day and senior football season were good enough to get me drafted in the late round or signed as an NFL free-agent, but my production up to that point was not. My resume lacked consistency, and I could not deny that. No NFL team wants to hear stories about poor coaching, immaturity, lack of commitment, or a great turn around when 1,000 other people vying for the same position have resumes that display consistency. That truth bothered me not because it cost me but because it was the truth. My production was not consistent early on because of what I did not do. At the same time, the overwhelming initial interest I did get on our pro-day was a result of what I did do.

The interest of multiple NFL Scouts showed me I was capable of being elite while informing me that working toward my vision had to remain a priority over an extended period. We all are more than capable of being elite, but few are willing to be consistent enough to reach that level. When I knew I would not be in the NFL I thought I missed my chance to be successful because I was only focused on my wants, but when I focused on God's wants for me, I saw all He had exposed me too and how He showed me what I was capable of. For many years I thought I was focused on the NFL, but the truth is I was focused on what I could gain from the NFL. I was chasing the life and not the difference the NFL would make in my life, my family's lives, and the lives of those I influenced. Chasing notoriety blinded me to a mentality I had not embraced and the progress I had not made. Being blinded and misled by notoriety enabled me to ignore the discipline of consistency.

As some teammates progressed, I was stagnant. Then as I began to wake up and invest more in myself as a player, I could not make the mental shift because the work I had not done would not allow me to believe in myself. By my senior season, my investment in the offseason gave me something to believe in, which led to a great season where I was selected Player of the week 4/5 games and named the Most Valuable Player (MVP) of the offense at the end of the season. A few months later I was in the best shape of my life by pro-day (Pre-Draft Workout for NFL Scouts and Coaches) and the most confident I had been since I was an incoming freshman. When the draft ended and months went by without a phone call, my focus went from chasing notoriety to simply being able to get paid to play. Looking back, when I finally accepted I would not be playing professional football, I never stopped to acknowledge that my consistent investment of effort over the last 2.5 years added more to the individual than it did to the football player. In failing to acknowledge what I had given of myself, I could not own who and what I had become to utilize the tools I gained right where I was. I knew my effort had set me apart at my pro day, but I did not realize it was not only my competition but also the old self that I had separated from. The work you are or are not doing sets you apart, but seeking your will versus God's will can make you completely blind to your reward through what He has done for you, in you, and through you by selfishly looking at your progress in reference to what you are seeking in personal gain.

Consistency Creates Separation

Do you see your blessings or your transgressions? The mental and physical capacity we encounter on our journey reveals God's power and the power he has bestowed upon us; the strength, knowledge, talent, and gifts that confront us aides us in establishing a new normal. A new normal isn't turning away from who you are, it's embracing what you have become.

For example, when starting a new workout regimen, those first few days are horrible as you work to get in shape or get accustomed to the new routine. If you are consistent in effort, by week two the intensity of the workout still feels the same, but not as unbearable as week 1 (despite all the soreness). Then by week 3, you notice your fatigue setting in during the latter stages of the workout. Finally, around the end of week 3 or the beginning of week 4, you find yourself adding more weight or doing extra reps because the workout no longer has the same effect—you have established a new normal. You no longer come in focused on your soreness, dreading the workout, or upset about being weaker a month ago; you come in with a new mental approach based on the experience of building your strength and getting into better shape.

Outside influences disrupt our consistency and foster environments for our bad habits to flourish, but they are only impactful because of what we allow. Accountability is key to our new normal in that ownership leads us to focus on why we allow external influences to have more impact on our routine thoughts, speech, and actions than God's will. When we establish a new normal, old habits become unsettling because they are not in line with where we are headed. We recognize we are our own toughest opposition and the inconsistencies in our lives are a result of our choices. In fact, because of the demands and restrictions we place on ourselves in our new normal, everything and everyone that interferes with our ability to consistently progress toward God's will is questioned and/or removed as they become less appealing/influential.

As time passes by, when establishing a new normal, the degrees of separation from the old you and those you left behind are more prevalent. You may have experienced this starting a new job or taking on a new responsibility at your current job because leadership believed in you. Outside of work, this happens when you get that itch or tug at your heart that you need to be doing more with your life, so you dedicate more time to being productive, like working out, hanging out with people who have been where you want to go, reading, volunteering, going to church, or giving extra effort at practice or in class. Everyone has been called to something greater, so we all experience a push, a tug, or the itch, but few are willing to take action. The inclination to act, sustain, and grow is what you must take from your comfort zone to your new unfamiliar territory. The itch in unfavorable or unfamiliar circumstances does not go away, but your confidence in yourself may not be as high. This is when the discipline you developed and confidence you embraced that got you there must be enforced to break through. Here in unfamiliar territory, emotions battle our discipline for reign over our decision making. We can choose to let emotions win and settle or ignore our emotions to utilize our confidence and consistency to scratch the itch.

Emotions are public enemy number one to consistency because they make excuses and accommodations when we should follow our instincts. For instance, we make accommodations by allowing family and friends space in our lives that they don't deserve, which leads to compromising our routine. In these instances, the emotional pull to avoid conflict drives us to make a decision in our family or friends' favor so we can keep the peace or make them feel comfortable. There is nothing wrong with being flexible or available; in fact, we should lend ourselves to others, but we cannot be available to a fault. Instead of allowing their lack of discipline to influence us we have to allow our discipline to have a positive influence on them.

On the other hand the emotions that disrupt our consistency aren't always derived from a negative source. Sometimes we get overexcited, causing us to lose sight of our plans or core values. With one decision, we lose countless hours of sacrifice, strategy, and hard work. We see this often in entertainment or sports where an individual may be excited about a recent accomplishment and the decision to drink and drive causes that person to end up in jail or even worse, causes a fatality in an accident.

When you have your HeadDownPushing, relationship highlights a consistency that separates emotion and passion. We engulf ourselves in our passion without any push or requiring any compensation because it gives us life. Passion is often mistaken for an emotion because of their similar effect, but emotions are derived and true passion lives within us. We don't need motivation for our passion; our passion is our motivation. It gives us energy, keeps us up at night, and uplifts our spirit. While emotions have a similar impact, they are not the same and can be detrimental if mistaken. Our passion is given to us by God. Our emotions are a result of external and internal influence; therefore, they are inconsistent because emotions are preference driven. Passion on the other hand, renews our perception which not only changes our preferences, but also redefines the influence of our preferences on our emotions.

The stability of emotions varies from person to person, while passion remains consistent. We often make the comment, "I'm not as passionate about that as I used to be." We must be very careful with these statements because it is not always passion but emotion that was driving us and emotion that stopped us. In many instances when we perceive our activities as favorable, things could not be better, but if the activity changes or an element changes that we disapprove of, then we lose interest.

Many of us either experienced or witnessed this at work, in our eating habits, or fitness goals. In the beginning, we are excited and on a high about the thought of changing our health/fitness lifestyle. We go out and buy equipment, new clothes, gym memberships, and even supplements. We get started with the new workout/meal plan, then suddenly whether it is bad weather, a tough workout, soreness, the temptation of food not on your meal plan, or simply being tired, the perception of our new lifestyle shifts.

If not fitness, think about that dream job or career change that was going to "change your life". You always envisioned the salary, the glamour, the title, and the allure of the perks you associated with the position, while overlooking the day-to-day requirements to attain the position, keep the position, and be successful in the position. After a few months or so of redundancy, extra stress, lack of support, and lack of fulfillment, that dream job became a nightmare or that new career was not worth the toll it took on you each day. When our perception shifts, you lose touch with those emotions that created your enthusiasm. This happens more than we like to acknowledge because many of our actions are driven by our emotion. Instead of acting on emotion, we must be driven by the source of passion that jumpstarts our emotions. When we focus on our passion and use it as our source of energy, we are more rational, patient, and committed to seeing things through because the consistency of passion keeps you grounded and focused on fulfilling your assignment.

Pushing people beyond the limits they have accepted, by being courageous enough to believe, trust, and invest in themselves is my passion. Leading and encouraging others is something that always came natural to me, but I had no clue I was passionate about people overcoming the odds in their lives until I did a deep dive into my own emotions to understand what was stopping me and what drove me through that opposition. After college, when I had no outlet for my passion, I began to channel that passion in other areas such as mentoring, coaching/training, social media, blogging, public speaking, conference calls, and ultimately writing this book. I never said to myself that I want to be a speaker, influencer, or author I was just trying to be accountable to being that consistent voice that showed the people I love I believed in them because I wanted them to ask more of themselves. At the time I would've told you I didn't like writing. Now writing is something I really enjoy when I feel I have something to share that will help others. It is a pretty simple task on social media, but it takes an overwhelming amount of work to take those thoughts and turn them into a book. The process of dumping all my thoughts, restructuring those thoughts into chapters, developing those thoughts with supporting stories/content, updating the content to official book format, then editing, editing, and editing is not the most exciting thing to do. As a matter of fact, I've been on a roller coaster of emotions the past few years in regards to how I felt about staying at work late to work on this book, coming to the office on weekends to work on this book, staying up until it was almost time to get up for work to work on this book, and waking up early/not sleeping on weekends to work on this book. I had no clue of what I was getting into, but I am committed to learning all the way up to and through the process of releasing and promoting this book. The frustration of time invested, lack of time, not knowing what to write, not knowing how to write, lost files, lack of knowledge, other interests, commitment to finishing, isolation, and doubt have beat me up over and over. What keeps me going is the passion that God placed in my heart and the responsibility I have as a vessel to give my contribution to those He has entrusted to me.

Initially I began working in the Healthcare field to just have a job that could possibly lead to more opportunity. The problem was I didn't know what a good opportunity was nor did I know how to prepare for it. In my first jobs I just came and went each day hoping someone would notice me. As I realized I needed to take ownership of my direction I saw how critical it was that I was consistent in being intentional about changing my circumstances. At this point

I've been working hard in the same field for over 10 years now to build a career and establish a way of life for my family. Direction provides the path, but it is up to us to make the investment. Investing in yourself requires patience because investing means to put value into something with a purpose; the greater the purpose, the greater the investment. One important factor about investing is that the investment is not for others to see, the investment is for you to own. It took some time, but I realized while I was learning an industry I was learning about myself as well. The more I invested the more I was empowered and the hungrier I became for others to understand the importance of investing in themselves. The young man "trying to get it" was now consumed with leading others out of an old way of thinking into learning how to build something that outlasts them.

I never really thought about legacy before because I was consumed with what I wanted to achieve instead of understanding my responsibility to build upon what was passed on to me. Once again I was being redirected as life charged me with honoring what was sown into me by building for those who come after me. The words building and legacy both strike my attention because of the responsibility they imply. So I harness that energy and apply it to my passion in order to be intentional with my time. If I'm not intentional with my time I'll dedicate all my time to building someone else's legacy instead of building my own. So know when you think about legacy, it doesn't matter if you can trace your legacy 6 generations or none, to kings & queens or strangers & adopters if you aren't intentional about where you're headed. Building requires consistency that creates a transformation. A few years ago I was simply posting on social media, now I'm writing this book to build legacy.

My progress today is a part of my consistent intentional effort to not accept being a pawn, but working to own the Chess set. Career building created a long-game discipline in me that sports and school could not provide. The inconsistencies of the working world remind you abruptly and harshly that you are expendable so it is up to you to know how to continue to add value to yourself as life forces you to adjust. You have to know where you're headed with or without your employer because they are headed somewhere and it may be with or without you. We see this in professional sports all the time when players are released or cut from the team. It is their responsibility to be prepared for whatever decision the team makes in regards to their future. If you wait until your employer acts to start contemplating your future…you're too late. In school players have the safety net of knowing they cannot be cut on top of the false sense of purpose that the structure of the program provides. What students/athletes have to take away is the discipline it takes to add value to yourself that you deploy in school or sports. You can't focus on what you don't know or what you can't control, you have to put your energy into being a sponge to soak up all the information around you whether it is direct or indirect. You can't afford to sit around and wait for someone else to make decisions about your career you have to be intentional about the information, the relationships, the exposure, the studying, and your execution. There will be days that you only see what's in front of you that frustrate you because you can feel it sucking the life out of you. The key is to not suffocate yourself in pity or negativity because the opportunity to add value is constant and you don't want to cost yourself tools/knowledge because you slipped into a routine of being negative or complacent when you should've been being intentional about building.

Through being consistent in my effort in writing and relationship I've learned that passion helps you create a pace and learning your pace is essential. Work, kids, wives, faith, and passion all require time. Balancing my roles and my investment in these areas creates a lack of time to invest in myself and my passion. When my lack of time causes lack of production it is defeating and depressing. This is a very sensitive place because feeling defeated turns in to losing (negative) thoughts and losing (negative) behavior. Before you know it one instance fuels a negative thought turns into a chain of bad decisions. When the truth is, dedicating time to serve in any of your roles is a win that should be celebrated then carried into the other areas of your life. This is why you have to learn to trust the pace your passion creates. As long as your pace is derived from your passion it's okay to prioritize or accommodate other passions i.e. family and service because that time away for others only incentivizes your execution.

Pace has nothing to do with speed or volume, pace is a rate which has everything to do with our consistency and obedience. I know those long nights of writing after playing with the kids and spending time with my wife count, those early mornings when I could've went back to sleep count, the time a take away from my family to go in the office on the weekend counts, the miles traveled to speak for free count, the integrity to stop writing for extended periods of time to go live and experience more for authenticity and truth in my writing counts. Emotions suggest, "you're window has closed" "you won't finish" or "no one cares", but passion says "if only one person is helped", "when my kids see what discipline produces" or "this execution is for inspiration". So I don't allow emotions to disrupt me by focusing on the time I don't have because this is my life. I just stick to my pace of honoring the time others won't by attacking it with everything I have.

Consistency creates discipline, discipline promotes execution, and execution creates results. All are a piece of your message. The execution that others praise is a byproduct of who you are (in your new normal) resulting from the lifestyle of discipline that you embody when you consistently strive for excellence in all things. Sports teach us mediocrity is guaranteed, but excellence is a result of our consistent intentional efforts. The same is true in our personal lives. Whether you're in a downtown office or you're a member of a late night cleaning crew, those who equip themselves to only accept excellence expose those who aren't opposed to mediocrity. When someone is acknowledged or pushed to the forefront because of the level of excellence they have maintained, and you feel exposed, you shouldn't perceive it as them seeking to intentionally hurt you, you should see it as them intentionally helping themselves.

When Kobe spent countless hours in the gym prior to others coming to practice and when they left the general public rarely heard about it. Then as Kobe began to separate from his peers and surpass them in regards to production on the court many of them were offended by the praise he received. While a few players angrily questioned public perception others knew to question themselves and their own investment.

Most people are either completely unaware of or conveniently forget the cost of success. This is why we witness countless individuals, seeking instant-results, fade with failure. On top of that, too many people have bought into the idea of "fake it, till you make it". This trend of selling success has so many people perpetuating lives they aren't truly living that it not only hurts the target, but also the perpetuator because the focus on the lifestyle makes everyone ignore or forget the cost of being successful. As they focus on manipulation and how they are perceived more and more people sell pieces of themselves until they are forced to give up on their dreams because there is nothing left to sell. If you look into their investment you'll find they decided to give up after they went on social media then randomly posted an idea, product, or get-rich-quick scheme and their post did not receive the amount of likes they wanted.

This type of routine is evidence that we believe in the gimmick more than we believe in ourselves. When we think this way we are saying to ourselves, "my character hasn't provided me anything tangible that represents the success I'm chasing. So what are they doing that I need to do to get what I want?" At this point it's a longshot if compromising our character is even an afterthought because we are consumed with it getting what we want. Think about the evolution of foolishness and warped moral compass we've witnessed from slapping strangers on video, degrading photos, and sharing of explicit content with no regards for ourselves or the receivers. We are so consumed with self-promotion and/or gratification that being the originator of information or center of attention trumps our values and belief systems.

There are also changes in patterns from those we respect when their intent is misguided. I have experienced this myself in my growth as a person of influence. It was after I posted a photo of the first HeadDownPushing t-shirt I received as a gift from my wife to help me grow my platform. In response I received numerous requests for shirts. I didn't have a website, I was unfamiliar with PayPal, and most importantly selling shirts was not my passion. But, the response put dollar signs in my eyes and in that moment I was distracted. The response was so surprising that my focus of how to distribute and sell more shirts grew with each day until that became my priority over encouraging others. When selling shirts became my focus I became so engulfed that I completely stopped posting because, I would be frustrated with being out of sizes, only having one color, not having a website, and perplexed with the amount of people saying they wanted a shirt, but only a few actually buying.

A few months later as I was discussing what was going on with me being a speaker, a friend asked about the shirts and I just remember saying "Man forget them shirts…I don't care about no shirts! They had me tripping! It won't be until I can build the brand up enough for someone else to manage all that again because that turned into a distraction for me." It was like an epiphany when it came out, because I hadn't realized how off-track I was when I was trying to sell those shirts. As I drove home I thought about how my intentions changed when I was engulfed in selling the shirts and how I stopped posting and reading to build myself because I was putting my energy into figuring how to sell the shirts.

Focusing on the wrong things makes us engage in schemes or ploys to fast track our lives or supplement our self-esteem. What we fail to realize is what we often consider an overnight success is actually the result of someone doing exactly what we're not willing to do—be consistent. Don't fail yourself by only seeing the lifestyle/results and disregarding the investment and don't sell yourself in order to sell a gimmick. It is up to you as an individual to study the cost to get to the top and use that as inspiration, motivation, and guidance for your investment of time and energy to create results. If we only see the glitz and glamour, we fail to see the role of consistency in creating the invaluable principles winners embody that serve as the foundation for their success.

Your faith is your source to sustain the consistency required to establish discipline. As you separate from you through this new discipline you get closer to Him. Relationship does not harm your effort, relationship empowers your effort. As you see more of Him and less of the old you in your being, you become more opposed to letting you get in your own way because your cost will never add up to what He (Jesus) already paid for you.

With that, there is greater separation in the person you are versus the person you're becoming. This is why excellence is so tough because you find yourself alone where few have traveled and you must learn to navigate on your personal path through faith. Hard work is a moniker that people throw around a lot because it's an expectation. Extra effort is even more common than it has been in the past, but consistent extra effort creates separation from pretenders and the old you. Whether you desire a little more from life or a complete transformation of your circumstances you have to submit yourself to the process of changing your life (this is the cost). The destination determines the workload, but it is your willingness to consistently show up and work spiritually, mentally, and physically to get you where you truly want to be.

Chapter 8

ACCOUNTABILITY

Bearing Responsibility for Your Actions and the Impact They Have on All that Has Been Entrusted to You

When we discuss accountability, we must understand what we are responsible for, why we are responsible for it, and know we have been entrusted because we have what it takes to fulfill the assignment. In understanding what we are responsible for, we are forced to first analyze our perspective so we fully comprehend what God has assigned to us. Our thoughts are the source of the success, failure, peace, restlessness, joy, misery, death, and life, which we experience and share with others. And as powerful as our thoughts are, they are our responsibility. This is why our perspective must be a Godly perspective, because His perspective enables us to understand all that we are responsible for, the value of all that has been entrusted to us, and the power of our influence on those things. This doesn't mean we strive to set ourselves apart through perfection, it means we strive to submit to our roles utilizing selflessness and service to honor all that has been entrusted to us.

Information and exposure are critical to our perspective because they are where our thoughts are derived from. So many factors play a role in what we are exposed to and what we believe as we grow up that it is unfair to assume or operate as if everyone thinks the same. Simply put, life is not fair, but regardless of the tilt of the playing field, we still have the freedom and the power to choose the direction of our lives. A huge problem with choosing is that life can be so dark and overbearing that many people don't even know they have a choice, let alone the power to choose where their life is headed. Information provides knowledge or makes us aware, fueling imagination, curiosity, and visions of life beyond our limits. Exposure takes information a step further by bringing things to life, making what appeared fleeting or unrealistic attainable. The seeing, hearing, feeling, smelling, and learning of new things plants seeds of dreams, goals, and ambition in our heart and our mind. If we don't act on them soon enough, we have to fight to suppress the internal desire to pursue those things.

Without information, our minds remain closed to the world outside of our household or community, and without exposure, we lack that spark that questions "why not me," despises settling, and drives us to seek more from life outside of our circumstances. As we grow older and learn the power that information and exposure have on our thoughts, we must accept the responsibility of seeking them to continue to evolve our perspective. When our perspective changes, we gain insight and appreciation for the value of all that has been entrusted to us.

The ignorance of our ability and power creates the inability to accept full responsibility for our circumstances. Instead of challenging ourselves to change our environment, our poor perspective encourages us to find excuses to validate how we see ourselves as our truth. When we identify as inferior, we think inferior thoughts and lead our lives as inferior people.

Culture has embedded in our being a rating scale that only considers factors such as income, race, social status, and sex. Ignoring that rating scale is a key component in understanding how great we are; otherwise, we operate as if we are not valuable or significant. Immeasurable value exists in every person; your passion, your determination, your gifts, your demeanor, your talent, your family, your friends, your thoughts, and much more have all been entrusted to you as a vessel to protect, to preserve, to share, to encourage, and to influence. But when we don't embrace our own significance, we cannot embrace the significance of others, much less comprehend the seriousness of our role of being accountable for contributing to their growth and progression.

The focus on celebrities in society pushes us to diminish how much it means to be a gatekeeper, a shoulder, a teacher, a mentor, an ear, an example, a reminder, and a trigger, causing us to lose sight of the roles we play in each other's lives. Without the people who fulfill these roles, many of the superstars we know today would not be in the position they are in. Don't devalue your position or your role; embrace your own significance regardless of your status, race, income, etc. The treasures that the world possesses should not seem exclusive or impossible to groups of people because of class, race, sex, religion, or location. In fact, those treasures are secondary to the true treasure that resides in each and every individual. If no one informed you early on of your responsibility for all that has been entrusted to you, you must leave that in the past and bear the responsibility of seeking information to change your course. Then take it a step further and be the role model you didn't have. The experience you have to share is invaluable for those who will not get it elsewhere.

The people who cared, fed, drove, compensated, loved, prayed, supported, acted, believed, encouraged, reminded, inspired, motivated, acquiesced, sacrificed, fought, risked, and much more are commonly undervalued and not mentioned enough. We spend too much time focused on the few that lied, stole, did not show up, used, abused, and disregarded us. The contributions of true treasure to our lives, whether it was one person or one thousand people, should indebt you enough to be accountable for the next person. I remember many occasions the impact of someone believing in me when I didn't. Whether it was my wife not letting me quit the Master's program, my mom challenging me to start living again, a friend asking me "What are you going to do," or my bosses forcing me to stretch as an individual, their belief shined light into my darkness and made me believe in myself. I value everyone in my life whose energy suggested I have something significant to contribute to the world. Their willingness to shine their light in my life encouraged me to forge on when I could not find the strength to do it for myself. That is the power of accountability, and I am forever grateful for them transferring their power to me.

Accountability brings about a vicious game of tug of war as we shift from the need to validate ourselves to the need to serve. Most of us go through a natural maturation process where *me* becomes a smaller priority and we, they, or those issues become a bigger factor in our decision-making. Still, as men and women, we find ourselves conflicted and torn as we deal with the selfish internal pressure to validate or assert ourselves, our thoughts, and/or our beliefs. We have to focus on being at peace with serving and doing what is right, knowing our compensation will be returned with interest. It is very easy to lose this game of tug of war, as you are unlearning the process of keeping yourself at the forefront. Be mindful as those self-serving thoughts try to creep in, be patient in your circumstances, and be a selfless servant who knows impact, influence, and results speak louder for you than you'll ever be able to speak for yourself.

Are You a Servant of a Cause or a Leader of an Agenda?

This question identifies your motivation and what/who you prioritize being accountable to. Serving a cause focuses on serving others, while leading an agenda focuses on serving yourself. In leading an agenda, you lead a lifestyle that disregards others to obtain what you perceive as valuable. In serving a cause, you bring things to you through valuing and adding value to the lives of others.

Submitting your life to a cause reshapes your total being. You begin to notice a difference in your approach to life as service reprioritizes your decision-making and reinvigorates your determination. Others are impacted as well through witnessing your growth or transformation through your authenticity, respect for, and commitment to who you are and what you do. They are able to see that true accountability is not selective. There is no picking and choosing when where and how; you just submit your all in the moment, accept all that comes with it, deal with the good and the bad that results from it, and move on to the next task when your work is done. When your heart is in the right place, witnessing an individual submitted to a cause affects you and makes you question what is truly driving you. Whether it is helping where you are or stepping in where you once ignored, you no longer are comfortable with not doing, because service is infectious in the spirit.

As I have grown older, observing the service of my parents has really revealed my own selfishness and pushed me to choose less favorable tasks more often to be of service to others. Many evenings, my dad would talk about how busy his day had been and how tomorrow would be a continuation. Then the phone would ring and my dad answered, "Hey, how ya'll doing? Really? Okay, I'll be down there as soon as I can and get that taken care of. What, no, no, you know you don't have to worry about that." After that he might make a phone call or two to reschedule his clients for the morning, and then he made the 2.5 to 3-hour drive to Corpus Christi that night or early the next day to do some work for family and not consider taking a dime. He then loaded up and jumped right back on the road and into his plans for his paying clients 2.5 hours away. He never let money get in the way of serving his family. He never considered the possibility of losing a job or client over serving those that had been entrusted to him.

The same goes for my mom. My brother and I witnessed her constant sacrifice to be the parent she was required to be for us. No job, no friend(s), no hobby, nothing ever kept her from being a presence that held us accountable. On top of that, she was that same presence to our friends and other youth in our town. She never treated anyone as "who they were" she treated them as "who they could be." That took courage in a town where many people frown at you for not looking down on others they had given up on. I remember my friends saying, "Say fool, we just saw yo mama in Mrs. Whomever's class." Then my closest friends and I scattered in fear in the opposite direction to avoid whatever trouble was to come. She would catch 1 or 2 of us always, but the worst part was going through the rest of the day not knowing what my teachers had told her. In still, after whatever talk we had about where my actions had brought me, she made it a point to let me know it would be my actions that changed my situation. We still laugh about her school visits until this day. And the amazing but funny thing is, she continued to do the same thing to a few friends when I had left for college. I did not even have a clue, but when I found out, I laughed because I know they were not ready for that confrontation.

Many of us are indirectly and unknowingly taught to live selfishly, then we pass this way of life down to our children. This behavior relieves the recipients of the responsibility of contributing to society by sheltering them from the time and effort required to serve. This is not a knock on anyone trying to provide a life for their children that they never experienced, but it is a reminder that service works both ways. Providing for others builds hope in those you serve and builds your character.

We cannot let service be foreign in our families and communities because of the value of others and the value you possess that service implies. Ignorance is bliss though, right? Since we have not truly experienced service, we may know we should be doing more for others, but we allow inferior thinking of "why we can't" to influence our actions more than our passion to serve. What has been entrusted to you? Who has been entrusted to you? Have you realized the severity of your absence or is it just too inconvenient to be a presence? At some point, you must stop finding excuses to remain content and be accountable for the fact that you can add value where you are with exactly what you have. You don't need to gain to give; you give first to gain what you need.

The burden of service can be a deterrent because "how we think" pushes us to consider where we lack first. This thinking brings us back to the me-first agenda. Most of us cannot see past ourselves to serve something other than our own agenda. We get inspired, motivated, and excited about lending of ourselves, so we begin with great intentions, but the inconvenience of serving quickly sets in, overwhelming our excitement and pushing *me* to the forefront. Many would argue that various factors stopped them like lack of resources or timing, but weighing more heavily are pride, ego, fear, and/or selfishness. Instead of focusing on how others will benefit from the service, their focus is the cost they aren't willing to pay. Whether it's inexperience, lack of engagement, lack of award, or looming criticism they aren't willing to endure in order to serve someone else's interest. In these moments you must ask yourself if giving to others is the priority or how you look giving it.

Being a wholly submitted and available servant to a cause rather than a leader of an agenda frees you to experience God's will. The cause, which is an identified need or issue, tugs at our hearts and consumes our thoughts until we act. In acting, we are blessed with revelation in our service. What is revealed to each individual cannot be defined, because God has a specific intent from person to person. But without the pure form of submission and obedience, we cannot have revelation, because our minds are focused on a self-serving agenda. Relationship keeps an open channel to the Holy Spirit to hear, see, and feel God's will in every situation. The self-serving focus of an agenda closes that channel because the focus is on me and not serving others. If we are not open in perception, operation, or in our overall being, then we cannot receive what God has for us in our service nor can we become what He has intended in this portion of our journey. Our lack of submission hinders us because we are blinded by our agenda. If we are not submitted in presence and effort, we forfeit the experience of our power for ourselves and others as the vessels we are in Him.

Don't Diminish Yourself; Respect Your Position

If you ask, most people will tell you they feel responsible to be successful, in part, because of the sacrifices made for them to get to where they are. While this may be true, most people are misguided in their goal to show appreciation or pay it forward. Some familiar goals are to "raise my kids in a different environment" or simply provide more on Christmas morning because "Christmas was just another day for me growing up." These desires are admirable, but they should be considered milestones or byproducts that are a part of your lifestyle or the environment you create by changing how you think.

The ultimate goal is to remove the unconscious lid off your vision and share that mentality and/or experience in the lives of those who have been entrusted to you. That is being accountable; empowering someone enough to change how they themselves and where they are headed. The sacrifices made for us were not for us to simply own things; the sacrifice was made so that in our thinking, "having things" is an expectation based on who we are. A big house is too small for where you are you headed; a nice Christmas is up to you, but empowering others to change the narrative of their life…that is purpose fulfilled…that is accountability.

The power to control how we think means we all have the power of choice, and with this power, we must be accountable to what has been entrusted to us.

As I stated earlier, the main issue with the power to choose is most of us don't know or will not believe that we have this power and many of us are so far down a path of self-destruction that we will not allow ourselves the time to understand, exercise, and be accountable to this force.

At the end of my junior year in college, I had come a long way from the carefree guy shying away from the urge to step up. I was no longer accepting what was and dedicated my time and effort to what could be. I could only imagine what the upperclassmen who came before me would think of who I had become and who I was becoming, because this Marques did not exist among them. They witnessed the Marques who struggled with immaturity and selfishness. My rough patches include being the guy with a bad attitude, getting benched, and even being suspended for a game only two years prior. I'll never forget the moment when I hit rock bottom. "Marques! Coach says I'm in," a teammate said, jogging onto the field after I failed to make a play. This was in the 1st quarter of the A&M game in my sophomore year. I sat on the bench the rest of the game until the final minutes of the 4th quarter. Then one of my teammates on the phone with our position coach said, "Marques, you in." "What! Man, fuck him!" I replied, feeling embarrassed and disrespected that he would even suggest I go in for garbage time. My teammate replied, "He says take the phone," extending the sideline phone to me. "Man, fuck him," I exclaimed one last time, waving my hand so he could see my gesture from the press box as I walked away. My teammate said the conversation continued when I left, "He didn't do what I think he did he?" my coach asked. "Coach, you take it for whatever you want," my teammate replied, trying to distance himself from the situation.

Later, after the game, my coach stormed into the locker room with a scowl on his face, flush from the Texas heat, and tried to reprimand me by berating me and bullying me, but at that point, I was emotionless because I no longer heard him. Over the 2 years that I had known him, I never felt he saw me as a person. His tantrums and rants had become so routine that they turned into a form of background noise at practice. He never connected with me and I never felt he had any desire to. So when he came into the locker room, I was already numb because I felt like he was not talking to me; he was talking to who he perceived me to be. Somewhere during his attempt to stroke his ego and reassert his authority, he said I would be suspended the next game. But I was so numb I did not understand what I had done, nor did I care.

As the following days passed, I thought more and more about my actions and the embarrassment of being suspended. Even though I felt wronged and knew he had previously mistreated me I did not have the right to be disrespectful to my coach. If there was a slither of space for me to display behavior that said I am not the guy you assume me to be, it was in this moment and I failed. I failed because I had allowed myself to become exactly what I feared, a selfish, disrespectful, ungrateful, knucklehead (exactly how he saw me). I forgot who I was because of how I felt I was treated. Since I felt I did not matter to him, I acted recklessly, like I did not matter, which only led to me hurting myself. That day was the validation of how lost I was. I was not accountable to anything or anyone, not even myself.

In these tough times, we must stay accountable to our morals, beliefs, values, and principles because this is when we grow; this is when we make a difference in our lives. This was a lost opportunity, but it was also a chance to reflect and be more prepared for future adversity. The coaching staff was fired that season, but that was the least of my worries. I was more focused on the work I had not done thus far and the negative impact I longed to change because I recognized the value of the opportunity and regained respect for my position and for myself.

Fast forward two years to fall camp, before my senior year began, when I received my most cherished award. I was voted by my teammates to be a Team Captain. I set out to be a leader, to make a difference, and to impact my teammates at Baylor as soon as I signed my scholarship, but I had fallen short years prior. Nine months prior to fall camp, I decided to rewrite my story. I was so fed up with lackluster performances and lack of presence that I challenged myself to focus on the shortcomings of my game and rededicate my focus, my consistency, my leadership, and my commitment to that initial goal. That entire offseason I was at the front of every line and went through every drill, exerting every ounce of energy I had into leaving the old me behind and setting the tone for everyone around me. My commitment was to leave Baylor better that I found it and leave something behind in my teammates that the upperclassmen before me did not care to leave in me.

Running sprints at the end of a morning workout during offseason is almost guaranteed. In between sprints, coaches routinely yell at the players to not bend over because it is a sign that you are fatigued or broken by the work. When culture is shifting, with time, coaches learn they don't have to police players because players take ownership (Accountability is infectious). Instead of bending over at the waist, I would squat between reps because I could breathe better in this position. Instead of fighting to keep my torso upright standing tall I would go right into a squat position with my chest up to recover as quickly as possible for the next rep. This is something I learned and adopted from my best friend, around the 10th grade, as he squatted anytime we stood around. One day I squatted down to say something to him as we worked through conditioning then I stood up for the next rep and realized my heavy breathing didn't last as long as it did when I stood tall. From that point on I would squat with my chest up to gather my breath quicker then stand tall until the next rep.

One morning, during offseason workouts, I walked back up to the line after my rep and squatted to gather myself as I encouraged my teammates and a teammate, who was new to the team, chose to call me out, saying, "Get up, Luling." I responded, "I'm good," because I knew he did not understand what I was doing. When I did not budge, he took it up a notch, imploring, "Stand up, Luling." At this point, I was offended. I knew he could not comprehend the 3 previous years of mediocrity and embarrassment I endured that I attributed to selfishness and fear. He did not know that I felt no one was more frustrated with below-average performances and losing seasons than me. I also knew that he had no clue that my frustration altered my investment. I played for me in the past, but now everything I did stemmed from my accountability to them, so my best was not just a goal, my best was my only option.

The coaches never challenged me on the squatting nor did the guys who went through the workouts with me as I set the tone by bringing everything I had to each rep refusing to succumb to fatigue and refusing to let them succumb to it as well. On top of that they all were witnesses to my changes; they saw my leadership, my resiliency, my sacrifice, and my investment…they honored the integrity of my effort and intent by pushing me to the forefront during offseason. Even our strength staff no longer kept tabs on me like years prior; they would focus on other groups because they knew my group was held accountable. So I laid into him before he could get another word out, screaming, "You don't call me out." My pace and voice gained intensity as I walked across the field to him. "You don't call me out!" I was ready to harm him if he confronted me. "You don't call me out," I said one last time for emphasis and reassurance that the message was clear. In the past we had guys who had not made the investment in the work or the people who would either yell to be heard or find targets they felt they could push around so they would be seen as a leader by the coaches. Knowing what the frauds looked and sounded like, I made it a point to be authentic and go with my gut versus doing what I thought a leader should do. I spoke with my actions first, I was inclusive of everyone, treated everyone with respect, and changed my habits. Sometimes you will encounter people who do not understand what it is to be accountable to something bigger than them. Their lack of understanding may cause them to react in numerous ways. You are accountable for the safety/reverence of the vision. You must learn and teach others to stand guard; to not allow an inkling of negativity to infiltrate what is taking place. I was not coming to my own defense, I was defending the integrity of what we were building; saying as a senior giving my all in every rep each day, *don't think to question my effort or my disposition as you all mean too much to me to choose to let you down.*

"I'm just saying, don't bend…" he tried to say, lowering his tone, looking for an understanding of his intent. But by this time my adrenaline was so high and before he could finish, I said, "I'm good, I'm good…you don't call me out." I stared him down before I walked back to my position in line, seeing that my message had been received by his reaction and altered approach. My teammates applauded and yelled "That's what I'm talking 'bout" "let's go Luling" as they began to channel that energy into our last sprints/drills and nothing else was said because my position and my commitment to bear the responsibility were defined. Seeing your dedication and commitment to your position changes the perception others have of you and validate your level of leadership/authority when they have not experienced it or stepped into that position themselves. There was celebration and not opposition because my actions triggered a new level of respect for my submission to the team's progression that they experienced in my work ethic, how I pushed them, how I supported them, how I respected them, and how I respected my position.

During my initial years, I would often think, "I may not want to finish at Baylor." That thought evolved to, "Maybe Baylor does not want me to finish at Baylor." The new underclassmen had no clue what we went through under our previous coaching staff. I was on my second attempt at college football under the new regime and I understood there was no room for the old me. The old me was a product of dysfunction and selfish pride. The new me was wiser, stronger, and committed to honoring my opportunities by submitting to them because I had become all too familiar with the painful regret of missed opportunity. Being chosen to be a captain was very rewarding considering where I had come from. The selection, more than anything, humbled me, because I took it as my teammates saying to me, "We trust you, on and off the field as our leader, we believe in the person you are to make decisions that put our best interests first for us to be successful as a team and as men."

I called my mom that night and said, "Mama, they elected me to be Team Captain." She said, "What? I'm proud of you, Marques." After a short pause she said, "Well, you know, to whom much is given, much is required." I really soaked her words up that night and tried to wrap my head around my responsibility to my teammates. I was not okay with simply having the title; I desired to be a presence that made a difference in the lives of the people around me. As I analyzed my circumstances, I realized my first responsibility was to keep doing what I had been doing because my actions were a presence. Humility and hard work were the overwhelming reason why they chose me and changing would do more harm than help. One of the most important roles leaders have is to define the role and not be defined by the role. When a leader owns his/her position that is passed on and empowers others to do the same in their roles.

Before being named captain, I knew I was a leader from my past experiences. At Baylor, I struggled with seeing myself as the leader of these men and could not imagine that building a new culture for Baylor football was my responsibility. What position are you in versus the position you should be in? Don't let the intimidation or discomfort of doing what you know is right stop you from bearing the responsibility of changing your life and the lives of those you serve as a leader. When I decided to step up, I thought I was just working hard to right my wrongs and change the story that was Marques Roberts thus far, but I did not truly understand my position. I did not know the influence I had or who I was in the eyes of my teammates. That is scary because if I chose to go in the opposite direction, some people would have gone with me. In no way am I saying that my teammates didn't have a mind of their own. I'm saying that we are all leaders in our own right, so we must respect the position we hold in our homes, families, communities, and workplace because our actions and attitude can right a ship or sink it if we are not careful.

We cannot reduce who we are as individuals regardless of where we stand; we have to respect our position. I began to treat my opportunity differently because I honored it. I was aware of the lack of leadership I experienced as an underclassman and hated the impact not stepping up had on me because I told myself, "I am unqualified," "They won't listen to me," "They don't want to hear this from me," "I am not capable of being the one." Stop questioning yourself or counting yourself out as I did. Nothing is hurting you more than not believing in yourself enough to take action. Rise up to the occasion and meet the challenge. What God will do through you will surprise you and others.

You are the missing piece that can alter the culture of your church, team, family, employer, group of friends, social club, or non-profit. You are responsible for letting your gifts shine outside of your comfort zone. We are built up to a point in our comfort zone, but we are held accountable for carrying our confidence, experiences, talent, gifts, and perspective forward into unfamiliar spaces, as His vessel, to influence others to find a side of themselves they don't know while we discover a side of ourselves we have yet to see.

Years later, my younger teammates thanked me for being myself and not treating them like nobodies and for showing them what hard work looks like. They thanked me for pouring something good into them by simply bringing my best daily and providing them an example to follow to be successful on and off the field. They thanked me for encouraging them to be themselves and creating an environment where they did not feel they had to conform to be accepted. The acknowledgment and praise came as a big surprise because they are successful businessmen, successful entrepreneurs, successful professionals and successful professional athletes. I did not understand nor was I even aware of the impact at first, but looking back years later, relationship revealed my time was not in vain. Even though I did not make it to the NFL, my career was not a failure. While I thought I needed the NFL platform, I just needed to honor all that God had bestowed upon me and entrusted to me. I saw the influence, I saw the value, I saw the impact, I felt their appreciation, and this revelation informed me my life is a message.

You must ask yourself if you are truly accountable to all that has been entrusted to you. And if you are not owning your position, how can you ask for more when you are not accountable for what you have now? Our level of respect and regard reflects our understanding or lack of understanding of the value of everything that has been entrusted to us. Whether you are a janitor or an owner, the integrity of your work should mean something to you; if you are a manager, every person's self-esteem should matter; and if you are a CEO, every perspective should matter. Respecting your position provides a new perspective that teaches you to honor all that you own. Meaning, you no longer overlook, undermine, undervalue, or take for granted any talent, gift, instance, idea, role, person, employee, friend, spouse, sibling, parent, child, or any other relative that God has entrusted to you. You approach and handle them all with patience, love, and a thoroughness that implies significance and worth that teach and inform others to embrace and display the same as they learn the value of who they are and the significance of what they possess. The welfare of your loved ones, your talents and skills, relationships, staff at work, peers/siblings that look up to you, and your presence/charisma that radiates throughout a room are all invaluable and entrusted to you as a caregiver, counselor, mentor, teacher, and faithful steward to honor all that you cover.

Sometimes the internal pressure to be responsible removes the joy in the opportunity and adds the misery of a burden. Ultimately, accountability is a requirement, not an option, because of the magnitude of the impact of our choices. In order to experience all that God has reserved for us, we must be accountable to all that has been entrusted us. This work is a blessing, not a burden; this work is an opportunity, not an obstacle, but when we lack relationship, we don't understand the value of what the work of being accountable is doing in us. Relationship imparts a humility that creates a shift in us where the burden is released, the work brings you joy, uplifts, and inspires others, and in your attempt to honor, it becomes an honor, because your respect for your position reminds you what it felt like to fail to be accountable. Here is where you increase your capacity to be a blessing and be used to serve His cause that reaches beyond our vision, knowledge, scope, or anything we can imagine because of the immeasurable depth of the impact of His power through our obedience.

Chapter 9

PATIENCE

The Discipline to Maximize Your Effort Without Trying to Control Your Situation Over an Extended Period

In today's culture, patience has become a lost virtue. We are consumed with instant gratification, microwavable results, trending topics, and overnight success. Across all industries, you can find leaders searching for increased efficiency through reduced keystrokes and lag time. Every day there are new discoveries in technology, medicine, geography, and new talent in the entertainment industry that adds pressure to those who have yet to have their "moment" or trying to figure out their next move. That pressure pushes many to continue to work while others quit in the face of the same pressure because they cannot see themselves being successful on the same path.

No one has issues seeing the pinnacle and longing for that position, but only a few acknowledge, respect, and embrace the work it takes to get there. Your short-term goal of each day can't be driven by fame, money, or all that comes with success. Each day, simply focus on improving and being the best version of yourself by being in His will versus on your pursuit. The impatience we experience is a product of our intent to gain, which we have to counter by focusing on our responsibility to serve. When we are in

His will what we gain in service reveals how much we truly aren't prepared. Part of the reward that patience imparts is the understanding of His power in us and through us right where we stand if we are obedient and bold enough to get out of our own way. This is why it is critical to know who we are in Him and not be confused by how the world defines us or how we define ourselves. We all have something to contribute exactly where we are, but far too often we aren't even aware of our responsibility or capability because our faith and character in the form of willingness and intent makes us sell ourselves short in what we deliver.

Every morning before heading to daycare my very independent three-year-old son, Jackson, insists that he buckle his own safety belt while holding a cup of juice, a toy, an iPad, and a lunch kit in his hands. So daily, I tell him I will hold his juice and give it to him once I get in. This triggers him to say, "Daddy, I'm being patience (patient)" before I can close his door, insinuating he wants his juice even though he has yet to unload his belongings to take a seat. I then tell him, "Being patient means getting in and settled for both of us," as I begin to get in the car and get situated (which usually happens before he finishes). To which he replies, "But that is too wong (long), Daddy," leaving me amused about him and this routine.

When situations in our lives become overwhelming or things don't go as planned we are often like Jackson in that we cannot get back on track fast enough. This leads to irrational decisions in an attempt to force life to go how we want. If you have to force the issue, then people, circumstances, you, etc. will likely not be positioned to create the outcome or results you are seeking. My old receivers coach Harold Jackson used to say "Be quick, but not in a hurry." That meant act swiftly, but don't sell yourself or the play short by rushing and throwing the timing off. Football plays have timing like an orchestra. Once the ball snaps all positions have a responsibility and there is a timing component of each play. The lineman must set up and hold their blocks for a specific amount of time that allows the quarterback to take the snap then drop back to enough steps to reach a particular depth before throwing the ball.

The quarterback has to drop back to a specific depth to allow the receiver to reach the predesignated spot for that play. The wide receiver has to run a specific distance before breaking the route off and looking for the ball in order to be on time for the pass from the quarterback which also keeps the defender at a disadvantage. If the receiver rushes and cuts the route short the defender will have enough time to recover to stop the pass because the quarterback won't be prepared to throw the ball. There are multiple people who play a large role in a receiver being successful. Every play he has to trust his teammates to complete their task and be accountable to complete his despite not knowing where the quarterback will throw the ball. Some games the ball comes early and often and in others it may never come your way. The important thing isn't figuring out the defense as figuring out the defense becomes second nature over time. The important thing is training your mind to bring all of you to each play. You never know when opportunity is coming and all it takes is one slip in your patience that leads you to take a play off or not trust the timing and you miss your opportunity. In the same manner life has a cadence that is out of our control. We cannot afford to rush through or around issues, assignments, or opportunities to get what we want because rushing through life creates a lack of investment in time and energy that gets us out of cadence with God's will and the work He is doing to align our circumstances before us.

The number one sign of lack of patience for me is restlessness. Restlessness is leading a noisy lifestyle where we lack the clarity to make sound decisions. We bounce from what seems like endless points of contention to meaningless, thoughtless, empty activities to avoid facing the silence of our dilemmas and navigating our thoughts, desires, and pain in order to be productive. When I lost the structure that football and school provided, I became a busy person but definitely not a productive person. My time I was giving away to be immature, selfish, and numb was adding up to nothing. I had to step aside from the noise that was my restlessness, thoughtlessness, friends, and environment (which was any place I could find to distract me from facing my truth) to find clarity in my circumstances. I had to stop all the noise so I could gain perspective, establish a plan, and execute. Once again, I tapped into my faith to reinforce to myself that I was capable of doing better which came with a large dose of humility that made me be okay with where I was. As I navigated the silence, over time, I embraced the patience and focus I needed to wait on the return from investing my energy into working through my circumstances and not restlessly investing my energy into running from my situation.

Patience is the ability to become while God prepares or aligns the universe for what He has in store for you. Patience is where we develop the perspective to recognize opportunity, the courage to not avoid opportunity, the willingness to seize opportunity, and the humility to recognize we are accountable to a greater purpose in the opportunity. The understanding of God's faithfulness to us in each opportunity forces us to be consistent in repeating this cycle until His work is done. I was in a hurry, unaccountable to my responsibility for the play God called for my life. In rushing I was focused on where I wanted to be completely ignoring my assignment where I was. In being still I saw that even though my lack of patience showed I was focused on the wrong source, God never stopped being faithful to me. He is faithful to you as well, but you have to have the patience to fulfill your assignment to experience the glory of His play call for your life.

In the Bible, James 1:4 reveals that patience has a perfect work. We don't have a schedule of events for our life, which makes patience critical as the journey of life takes us to new places. Amid the delay between new endeavors or between peaks and valleys, we are responsible for becoming by patiently growing through the work in skill, knowledge, and relationship. Once again, through patience, we are prepared and opportunity is prepared for us. As we work in anticipation and expectation to prepare we have to remain cognizant that perfect work does not mean all of what we desired; it means all of what God desires. Patience is derived from His peace that stops us and starts Him. When I say 'stops us' it means we stop referring to ourselves and begin to refer to Him, better yet, we start and continue all things in Him. Our renewed perspective to recognize/identify opportunity and the wherewithal to work to get in position for opportunity are the results of being in His will. The work we do in patient anticipation of opportunity or the work we don't do in impatient restlessness enables us to experience the joy of His perfect work or the pain of our restless misery.

Earlier we discussed how gratitude leads to humility. These are the first two states we must reach before we finally arrive at peace. Once we have peace in our spirit, we can be still and see God's will in our circumstances. Peace provides clarity for self-assessment to understand where we should focus our energy for growth, for progress, and for preparation while we wait. We all get antsy for opportunity or that breakthrough moment when we have goals, but patience steadies us and prepares us to not only see the opportunity but also seize the opportunity. The specifics of your "time" or your "moment" are unknown, but what is known is that you must be prepared or that time never happens. Being prepared means you are aware enough to recognize opportunity and confident enough to execute in the moment. As previously mentioned, this level of confidence and awareness comes from the process, but it takes being patient in the process to be perfected, figuratively not literally, for the moment.

The patience peace provides in the process enables you to be content. This does not mean you settle in your circumstances, but you understand your moment has not come. You are content with growing in your current situation and progressing in your craft until that moment presents itself. This is the beauty of being in God's will. Patience provides clarity that you will never be fully prepared, but through Him, you will exceed expectations in the opportunities He has prepared for you.

Patience Is More Than Waiting

We are responsible for growth, which reflects discipline, consistency, and patience…all products of our choices. Too often in referring to patience, we use the word wait or waiting in its most literal sense. But the truth is, patience is more than waiting; patience is growing. If it is not our time to seize the moment, it is our time to focus on growing mentally, physically, and/or spiritually. Growth does not happen instantly; the only way we grow is showing up and giving our all to the work before us, whether it is a craft, trade, career, health, maturity, or faith. This is why clarity is essential. The clarity we gain in peace enables us to focus on the grind (work) and see the value of the effort it takes to reach our goals moving us past simply waiting with no expectation into working with specific intent.

One definition of patience is to be delayed. If it is God's will that we are delayed, then why wouldn't we take ownership in becoming the best version of ourselves in preparation for the end of the delay? This allows us to move seamlessly into working because when we can see the value of the process, we are actually seeing God's will. Therefore, we understand we are where He wants us to be. Instead of focusing on where we are not and what we don't have, we are grateful for where we are, what we have, and the expectation of the opportunity to come. Delay makes us focus on our schedules causing us to miss the truth that delay displays His control of time which we know will never be in our control. While we cannot control the time of our delay, we are in complete control of how we spend our time in delay. In seeing His power in and through delay, we are encouraged to use patience to control our delay instead of letting delay control us.

Too often, we confuse purpose with profession. We have purpose in every role we are entrusted, including friend, spouse, parent, relative, leader, employee, peer, sibling, and servant. Each role we own adds to the overall vessel that we are in God. As we work through assignments, we grow through witnessing our progression and the reward of work. We must be diligent in each role, as the lessons learned in one role trigger progression in our other roles. For example, being a better servant of God, pushes you to be a better man, striving to be a better man encourages you to be a better husband, being a better husband shows you how to be a thoughtful leader, being a more thoughtful leader informs you how to serve your children; serving your children makes you a more considerate friend, being a considerate friend makes you a better being.

Proverbs 13:4 says the soul of the sluggard desires and hath nothing, but the soul of the diligent shall be made fat. This verse teaches us that the reward is in the work, as the process adds to who you are in the Spirit, redefining your values and increasing your wisdom. The priority of this scripture is stepping out of our chaotic world to work at relationship as the scripture focuses on the word soul. It brings us back to the peaceful patience to diligently spend time, praying, reading the Bible, and being in His presence to grow in relationship and experience the fat (overflow) in the spirit. The overflow in the spirit spills into our lives aiding us to abide in His will. In His will our work no longer adds to our possession as a priority, it adds to our being first and the gain is a byproduct of the fat. On the other hand a lazy person has deep desires, but possesses nothing. They won't do the work in relationship robbing themselves of His of His peace and joy. The lack creates a dissension in their soul that steers them to dwell in destitution. As they wade in their suffering the laziness of wanting drives them to deflect responsibility instead of His peace leading them to work. The slacking costs them the experience of the growth and reward in preparation that we incur when our soul is made fat.

Diligence indicates patience, attention to detail, consistency, and resiliency that most are not willing to submit to. When your work builds your soul there is an investment that takes you to a depth that you have to work to get to, all while knowing, you have to work your way out. Too many people stop to look up and become overwhelmed by where the work could possibly be taking them.

They begin to focus on the what-ifs and not the requirement of the role/assignment. When we stay focused on the assignment our being locks in on completion as His vessel. The deeper we are taken the more we lose until it is only Him and us and the only place we have to reach is within. Where we are forced to reach within becomes base of the foundation or the core of the values we operate from. The patience required to build this foundation provides reinforcement of who we are in Him and the reward of working to do His will demonstrates no one can give you anything that will surpass what you receive in patiently working through the process.

Trying to Control What You Can't Makes You Lose Control of What You Can

If you are working out of a place of peace and not restlessness, your energy is never depleted. In fact, you often experience an overflow due to your efficiency. If you are operating out of restlessness, you run yourself ragged because you don't allow yourself to be renewed spiritually, mentally, or physically. Isaiah 40:31 states, *"But they that wait upon the Lord shall renew their strength; they shall run and not be weary, they shall walk and not faint."* The first portion of the scripture is straightforward in stating that if you wait on God, your strength will be renewed. The energy you have exerted in patiently building where you are will be returned to you for what is in store for you. The scripture also states that the hard work you put in builds your strength and stamina for your journey.

When you reach tough spots on your path, you will see others be weary and exhausted and you will be able to sustain a high level of performance without wavering. Becoming weary and overwhelmed are signs of restlessness and being outside of God's will. Restlessness does not allow you to be idle physically, mentally, or spiritually. The battle to control your circumstances consumes you, resulting in either not being able to sit still, constantly churning your mind to control what you cannot, and/or remaining unsettled in the spirit by focusing on what you don't have or chasing distractions. This is why many people don't have the stamina to run the race, why they walk and faint or run and become weary. Their impatience does not allow them to be content, causing them to exert all their energy and focus in the wrong places, robbing themselves first of the reward and secondly of the opportunity to build/equip themselves for their moment.

A restless person is one who has lost control and is endlessly searching for leverage. Anytime we are restless about any area of our life, we must first seek peace to have the clarity to make sound decisions as we go forward (For Christians, this is the peace of Jesus Christ). Being in God's will consumes us with peace, so when we recognize our peace is gone and we are unsettled we know we are operating outside of His will. When we are outside of His will the illusion of being in control momentarily settles us. I call it an illusion because even when your situation is as good as it has ever been you still have no control over where things are headed and unless all things considered are positive we struggle to navigate without peace.

We can only aim to be as prepared as possible for a shift in the market, in our department, or in our personal lives and then adapt to the new circumstances we are faced with. In the illusion of being in control, we try to control all elements and then panic when issues arise. Anything unexpected is perceived as negative, as the issues remind us we are not in control. The best leaders don't have the most control, the best leaders have the most peace and that peace enables them to remain calm when everyone else is up in arms. The knack to manage or tackle problems or perceived problems is a great characteristic of leaders, and this is what you see in the individuals rising to the top in all areas of life. If you are having trouble identifying whether you have peace, revisit how your last problem made you feel. In the illusion of being in control, the smallest hiccups disrupt your peace, but in His peace, issues are an expectation.

On the journey, impatience is a derivative of self-centeredness. If my intent is self-serving, then I become unsettled with delay, but when my intent is to please Him, I am able to work and rest in peace, knowing I'm where He wants me to be regardless of my circumstances. When my career aspirations began to develop (notice I said develop, because before I was just working) I just wanted more money. With time, I learned I would have to commit to progression to get in position for a position that received the compensation I wanted. My first thought about making the commitment was the time it would require, which meant patience was my only option.

I had a few hurdles in front of me because I lacked experience and education. So my first move was to become more knowledgeable of the industry to make me a more desirable candidate. My second (simultaneous) move was to work on obtaining my Master's in Business Administration to show dedication and meet the requirement of having a graduate-level degree to get into upper management. I was amid delay, but I did not let myself become restless, because clarity enabled me to see this as a part of the process. After about two years, I completed my Master's and received a "great for you" and a pat on the shoulder. I assumed I would get compensation, but that was not the case. So here I was newly married with a bonus-son, my new infant son, and no tangible evidence of progression in my career. That was a tough letdown, but I knew that was a minor detail in the major plan I had. Allowing that detail to command my attention and dictate my actions would be giving away the little control I had. Ultimately, I knew I could not control their decision about a raise, but I had total control of my actions beyond their decisions.

I didn't make any noise about my pay, I patiently worked harder and about 8 months into the position I received a promotion to supervisor after the previous supervisor left. This promotion came with a raise that I was grateful for, but I'm not sure if it even totaled a few hundred dollars annually. When I received the initial promotion, my own self-assessment told me it would take no less than two years to become who I needed to become regarding knowledge of the industry and developing the confidence to deliver. However, that would take pouring all of myself into the process I was committed to. I didn't even have time for the emotions of disappointment, I think I even laughed it off as I remained focused on the plan of becoming; because more than my employer's award, I was seeking God's will.

Right around the two-year mark, the tension between staff and management was at an all-time high and my patience was wearing thin. While a large portion of the management was being scrutinized, I was in the clear, but the battle to balance the relationships on both sides had become overwhelming. On one side, I was being pressured to reprimand my team. Anything from the time-clock, mistakes in processing work, break time, talking on the floor, and the list goes on. On the other side, the staff pointed fingers instead of taking ownership by dotting all their I's and crossing all their T's. My goal was to keep the respect/trust of my leadership while keeping the respect/trust of my team and my peers while sticking to my morals, but the balancing act was wearing on me. On top of all the drama, the pressure to make more money was becoming overbearing and by this time all I could think about was how bad I wanted to go.

My focus shifted from growing to going, and trying to control my situation only stressed me out even more. I would sit in the parking lot 20 to 30 minutes every morning because I dreaded walking into the office. I was completely miserable due to my lack of patience, I had lost control. One day I told God I had nothing left to give; the environment had broken me down to the point I could not be at peace. I asked Him, "What is left for me to do"? Then one day He showed me, "You have grown in knowledge of the industry, you have absorbed what it takes to be a leader in the workplace, but you still have my work to do." I realized then that it was not my job to juggle relationships but to reflect Him, to be the message. I realized it was my responsibility to stand up for what I knew was right and not let others avoid holding themselves accountable as well.

It was time for me to let Him use me by being bold enough to bring me to my role. Sometimes people need to hear the Gospel of Jesus Christ, in other instances they simply need to see the Jesus in you, and some need to be reminded of where their faith lies and their responsibility to be accountable to their beliefs. The relationships I had established made for a safe place for me to communicate openly from the heart how my faith steadied me and drove me to see me beyond my current circumstances. While I had spoken loudly with my actions, I was no longer in college, and as my mom let me know then, more was required. My voice needed to be heard to point out not only what was wrong, but point out our responsibility as individuals in these circumstances and to be the difference instead of contributing our energy to a broken culture. My intent shifted from staying in good graces with everyone to leading them to raise their own expectations of themselves, by being bold enough to be the vessel He called me to be. Shifting my focus revealed I was there as his vessel to demonstrate how to be the message and how to keep being the message a priority.

When my intent changed from serving me to serving Him, my peace was restored. I came in each day and sought to fulfill one thing…God's will. I realized that what work was asking of me was part of God's will, but because I had a plan (that I prioritized over His) I forgot I was on assignment. I had to let go of my own agenda, preference, and bias because I knew whatever circumstances I was to encounter, my assignment was to bring glory to Him. His will showed up in meetings with clients, executive leadership, quality assurance meetings with my team, and 1 on 1's with members from other teams. A few months past the two-year mark I set, two different employers offered me jobs with the opportunity to almost triple my salary.

Don't allow yourself to lose control by being distracted or depressed by delay. If you feel you are in delay, take a moment to examine your intent and how it aligns with God's will in your circumstances then ask yourself a few questions. How often am I passing up opportunities to grow by focusing on what I assume I am not capable of? How much has my effort and my time that I've invested changed how I see where I am, how I see myself where I am, and how has my time/effort changed where I see my life is headed? What has my selfishness caused me to overlook that God assigned to me (How much has what I want gotten in the way of what God wants)? Avoid the pain of looking back and seeing you did not recognize the opportunity to prepare for the opportunity to come because you were too focused on things that were out of your control. Don't just be…do with the specific intent of becoming. Patiently become where He has you in delay because what you allow yourself to become is the difference in where He is trying to take you and where you can't seem to work yourself away from.

Preparation Changes Perception

Preparation changes perception in that your perspective shifts because of your investment. I have discussed multiple instances of the work to become introducing you to abilities you did not know you have and relationship changing how you see you through submission. The work also changes how we see our obstacles. When we look at our opposition instead of seeing all the reasons why we can't, we begin to see the reasons why we can. A key factor in a changing or evolving perception is the transformation of our being as we begin to conduct ourselves according to where we see our lives going instead of according to where our lives have been.

Our perception establishes our expectations, our routines are birthed from our expectations, and we are products of our routines. High expectations push us to build routines that reinforce our significance and fuel our confidence. No expectations allows us to settle into routines that ignore our significance and accept our circumstances. Changing your routine begins with changing your perception. The only thing that has ever changed my perception is information. Information that I gathered from studying, conversation, observing, working, etc. It took an investment from me to go get or be willing to receive the information then apply it to my own life. Once I applied the information my routine changed because I began to operate in expectation. Here is where I began to see what others saw as challenges as opportunities. It didn't matter if the problem was random or expected, because of my investment I was willing to step up while others shied away. How are you spending your time? I'm not asking if you are prepared for a problem, I'm asking are you equipping yourself with enough information to be an expert in your respective role or field. Or when the next opportunity comes will you continue to be one amongst many avoiding a challenge that you feel you can't accomplish.

Most people in office settings feel the most intimidating meetings are impromptu meetings because there is no way to anticipate what may be asked. Scheduled meetings are less intimidating because you are normally given an agenda, giving you time to prepare answers and suggestions for improvement. However, showing up unprepared for a scheduled meeting causes high anxiety because the expectation is that you are prepared. Lack of preparation causes you to focus more on the possibility of failure instead of being confident in the investment you made leading up to the meeting. This lack of confidence often leads to assumed failure, which causes you to perform to the level of your own expectations.

Whether meetings are impromptu or scheduled, you must make it a priority to be consistent in your investment so you know the details, you are aware of the possible impact of your issues, and you are able to demonstrate you are confident in your ability to take action to do what is best for the department, team, company, customers, shareholders, fans, family, or anyone with vested interest. No matter your role in any scenario or profession as a traditional employee or an entrepreneur, it is your responsibility to develop a routine that creates a level of expertise in your being that you operate from in all your assignments.

Professional athletes often make plays in the most critical moments that leave fans baffled. Their ability to rise to the occasion comes off so naturally, as if they don't recognize the stakes of the moment. The reality is their actions are second nature because of the time they commit to recognizing the situation and turning up their focus for precise execution. Coaches dedicate extended hours to situational coaching and even go the extra mile in creating the atmosphere of high-stress moments by doing things like adding noise to practices, adding game-time elements such as the time clock, and even suggesting reward/punishment for successful execution. Recreating the atmosphere in practice changes players' perspective of the game time situation because they have seen themselves execute and succeed in these exact scenarios.

There are also numerous moments when athletes appear to make what analysts and commentators call a bad decision and it turns into a great play. In most cases, this is due to their investment leading up to those split seconds where they have become experts in identifying opportunity. The rest of us have no frame of reference, so we can't comprehend their thought process. Sometimes their decision is based on a skill they have sharpened for hours on end, instinct developed from years of being engulfed in the game, and in other instances, their actions are even based on tendencies they identified in hours of study sessions leading up to the game or something they picked up on during the contest.

At the professional level, all athletes are gifted, some exceptionally gifted, but the players who create the most separation between their peers are the players who make the most investment in preparation regardless of their ability. This is why we see athletes like Tom Brady, Kobe Bryant, Floyd Mayweather and LeBron James remain at the top for so long. Their investment turns them into experts at exploiting the weaknesses of their opponents. Talent, skill, and physical attributes are all factors, but preparation provides an element that enables them to either dictate or respond to in-game situations that confuse and overwhelm others.

Think about situations you have walked into blindly. There is always a level of discomfort or uncertainty because you don't know what to expect. You have to realize there will always be an unknown element or unexpected mishap, but preparation changes the level of impact of the unexpected. I am in no way suggesting that you can be prepared for the unexpected in every walk of life because that is impossible. However, if it involves, your role at work, a performance, a game, or any role that you own and have the opportunity to prepare for, you have absolute control over the investment you make. What you invest in preparation and execute in the moment not only builds your confidence but also builds the confidence others have in your ability to deliver. The investment of working to build yourself up and not waiting to be prepared not only changes your perception but also changes other's perception of you. When we are prepared, in the words of CBS' Big Brother, we 'expect the unexpected'. This is how the impact is limited, because our expectation and our routine has prepared us to rise up in the face of adversity.

In the face of your greatest challenges, relationship reassures you that every opportunity ahead is in orchestration for you. This perspective settles your spirit, providing you a peaceful confidence to invest in who you are in Him. Popularity, money, notoriety, and validation are all resisted and pushed aside as you become aware of how you allowed them to misguide you before. This peaceful confidence enables you to be deliberate and unshaken in your direction; empowering you to focus on what you can control versus being distracted by the elements that are out of your control. If you focus on the size of the obstacle or all the factors that place you at a disadvantage, you have lost sight of purpose. How is not your responsibility; you are only responsible for pouring your all into your work and He does what only He can with your investment. If you are being delayed for purpose, imagine God's perspective of the value He sees in your life. Embrace His perspective by patiently working and growing in relationship and then stay out of your own way by not choosing to simply wait or control what you can't.

CONCLUSION

The majority of us don't truly understand our power and our reach. The depth and magnitude of our influence is often overlooked or disregarded. Corporations have always understood this, which they have displayed in marketing and other communication strategies as celebrities are plugged in for their ability to influence. Whether it is clothing, cars, food, non-profit, etc., influence is accounted for in the marketing strategy. This power not only has the ability to shape the world we live in, but also has the power to change how others see themselves in this world. The problem with influence for individuals is this remarkable, immeasurable, and significant power is relative to our investment. The reason this is a problem is that the individual worlds we live in have trained us to think in a way that, in most cases, restricts our capacity to understand who we are, what we are capable of, and the significance of being accountable for making our investment. Instead of passing down the tools of greatness, the understanding of the limitless possibilities, the humility for the opportunity, and the selfless joy of sharing, we pass on the bias, the hurt, the pain, the fear, the prejudice, the pride, the ego, the brokenness, the envy, the selfishness, and the misery of not living the lives that we have been called to live.

In reading this book, many readers will do what they have become accustomed to and seek a way to relinquish ownership instead of accepting the responsibility for the lives we lead. Why don't we want this ownership? Perhaps because we are unaware, we don't believe in our ability, we fear the unknown, we are comfortable in settling, we operate from selfishness, etc. I cannot answer that question for you, but I can tell you there was a time I had no clue about my responsibility, then I was unwilling to accept that responsibility, and even after accepting my responsibility, I still find myself in my own internal struggle to reprogram all that I was previously taught and accepted as my truth.

Uninformed of the power of acknowledging and owning the value in who I was as a person, I allowed the world around me to tell me how I should see me, how I should lead my life and what I should strive for in order to validate myself. The issue with being uninformed of who we are is the lack of connection from your core beliefs/values to your vision. We grow up with these ideas of what the lives of "good people" or "successful people" look like, but if no one takes the time to connect the dots for us, we don't see how the character, the commitment, the consistency, the effort, the resiliency, and the reward connect. We don't break down the walls of perfection that are assumed, leading us to create unrealistic standards that constantly remind us we don't have what it takes to achieve the standards we have created.

At the same time, we have submissive mentalities, conformed behavior, fast money, and stereotypical ideologies thrown in our face daily, staking a claim on our identity. As we toe the line of "finding our way" and "doing what everyone else is doing", we fail to recognize what we are gaining through our journey; in turn we fail to make deliberate investments in ourselves because we don't understand how all of our experiences or investment contributes to where we are headed. Then one day life calls upon that guy or gal, who has been lying dormant, to show up, and you lack the confidence to be that person. So you make excuses or simply turn away from the opportunity because retreating is easier than dealing with the obstacles of asking something of yourself that you are not accustomed reaching within for. The feelings and emotions that create the anxiety and avoidance are signs that you have confined yourself to the comfort zone of the world you are engulfed in, avoiding any instances where that guy or gal may have to show up.

How much of your journey stems from conformity? How much of who you are is a result of the fear of falling short of who you believe you can be? I will forever be grateful for my parents instilling in me that there is more to the world than the world around me. However, living in a world where seeing/experiencing more is rare and uncommon calibrates our minds to operate within the confines that are reinforced to us daily through the actions of those closest to us, reactions of strangers to our being, media influence, stereotypes we've embraced, the routines we adopt and adapt to, indirect and direct conversation, uninformed assumptions, and assimilation. If you haven't, take time to consider what you've allowed to inform, mold, and affect how you have led and continue to lead your life. A few questions you can ask yourself are, "Do my decisions feel safe?", "How much influence did tradition have on my thought processes?", and "Did I allow fear or discomfort to turn me away from my alternatives?" Once you have an idea it's your responsibility to approach life with specific intent because being intentional helps us to stay in control versus allowing external influences from negatively affecting your days.

Each principle of HeadDownPushing requires an investment we may never have asked of ourselves or have forgotten how to ask of ourselves in specific areas of our lives. We must reclaim the space for influence in our lives and refuse to give up that ownership by being intentional. When I finally realized how my behavior impacted my life, I dug deeper to understand the why behind my thoughts/feelings that led up to my choices. In looking into why I saw the power of influence. Because our lives/culture come with authoritative figures (family, friends, entertainment, etc.), that constantly reinforce how and why we should think and live. I never considered His truth as my source for my thoughts or perspective; I operated from the lies I learned, accepted, and feared based on the authorities my world suggested to me directly and indirectly. Who or what is the authority that serves as your primary influence in how you think and how you lead your life? The problem many of us share is the lies we choose to operate from place us at a disadvantage because of the limitlessness we fail to embrace in our abilities and in the world to receive us.

Our behaviors and/or routines are a reflection of the reality we've accepted for ourselves. Relationship reinforces His truth that pulls us away from the lies if we allow it to do so. The challenges we encounter in working away from operating within the confines of the lies we've accepted is where we have to keep our HeadDownPushing because challenges push us to return to those behaviors. These are the moments where being the message not only changes our lives, but changes other's lives as well. As we grow and become more self-aware identifying the behavior is essential, but unlearning the behavior enables our being to refocus that energy into operating in a new state or frequency where we create experiences for ourselves and others (This is where God does what only God can do in and through us). Your goal may be unknown, your resources may be exhausted, your experience may be limited, but you have to require yourself to bring your best effort in everything you do. If you change where you stand, in regards to your truth, His perspective will move you out of your own way, not to pursuit things, to honor and walk in the present blessings that are your life. Don't focus on the principles as if they are a checklist to garner success; focus on your responsibility to welcome the joy that is imparted when you release your burdens through submitting to His will and focus on the doing that is being asked of you wherever you stand. His will, will reveal and reassure your becoming and your purpose in time through your faith and humility.

Faith

The world will be at odds with religion for years to come. Studies on top of studies veer down various paths and peer into depths of history that have yet to be considered. While the struggle of religion continues, faith holds true undefined, relentless, constant, and immeasurable. What faith looks like cannot be standardized or regulated, as faith requires taking action, being confident, passionate, deliberate, and determined. Faith is not stagnant, faith is not defeated, faith is not settled, faith is not fearful.

My faith is in Jesus Christ and God above. This does not mean your faith is invalid if you are a part of a different religion. Your faith is only invalid if that faith does not change how you see yourself, how you see the world, and how you approach life. True faith implores you to move and does not calm until you act. If you find yourself out of sorts, lost, miserable, frustrated, with nothing left to give, you must turn to your faith and identify where you got out of touch with the source of your faith.

How would you define faith? Better yet, how does how you see yourself, how you see the world, and how you conduct your life in this world define your faith? Faith first re-informs us, then redefines us, and lastly, pushes us to action despite our circumstances or doubt. As time goes on, it is up to us to engage more in our faith because the challenges of life get tougher, mentally, physically, and spiritually. The greater our relationship, the more we see our faith take control over our circumstances, reinforce our new perspective, and reestablish itself as the foundation of our progression. All it takes from you is the first step, and the reinforcement, support, pull, and fire of faith changes how you experience life, but everything it takes to make that first step must come from you.

Humility

Humility is an expression or state of gratitude evoked by faith and/or experience. Through faith, we are introduced to our true identity. In learning our truth, relationship incites a state of humility where we revisit and redefine past experiences. Since faith implies we are and we have all that we need; in turn, we are humbled because we know we are not worthy or deserving of all that has been given and entrusted to us. Humility tailors our new faithful perspective by changing the narrative of past experiences that we misinterpreted. As we allow humility to redefine our being acknowledging its power, pushes us to release the burdens we carry in the form of pride, ego, impatience, selfishness, arrogance, self-pity, pain etc. The burdens we chose to carry occupy space that we have to choose to give to God because those burdens stifle His peace from flowing freely in our being and in our lives.

When we have His peace, our ability to diagnose life as it comes at us is heightened because the stillness of His peace provides stability in our being that nullifies the influence of our emotions. Humility stabilizes your spirit so you don't get too high in good times or too low in bad times, but you remain grateful to move forward as a better-equipped person because of the experience. Our experiences throughout our journey, not only empower us, but also equip us to empower others. Once we realize and own that responsibility, instead focusing of ourselves we seek his will in whatever we are going through learn more of His truth as the lies we identify with are dispelled.

As humility teaches and reminds us of our own value, we learn that we cannot fully see ourselves without seeing the true value of all people. When we free our minds of the standards and prejudices of society, we see the power and wonders that God has done in each individual. Embracing the value of people raises our awareness of the value of time as we recognize all the missed opportunities our perspective cost us. Knowing our responsibility as vessels, humility fosters a state and environment where we commit to always being open to serving, learning, giving, and receiving because closed-minds devalue/disregard people, time, and the opportunities they represent.

Willingness

When I think of willingness, I think of selflessly volunteering yourself and your time, looking for nothing in return; I think of athletes sacrificing their bodies on the fields/courts to garner a win; I think of the discomfort and/or anxiety we all feel before standing up for what's right. Willingness represents the few who do when others won't or don't. Willing people are disruptors; they change things because they question instead of accept. As vessels, willing people prioritize His will and the readily available endless list of excuses that we find at every turn of life is not even considered an option.

A willing vessel has a great responsibility in that your being is infectious. Many of us are on or have been on teams that are toxic and fragmented because members are uncomfortable with the cultural norms. Still, we go against what we believe in due to our lack of willingness to face the challenge before us to create the environment we desire. The toxic environment we refuse to address leads to miserable mediocrity or failure. The sad part is, everyone wants better, but the unknown tied to addressing the issue is a greater influence than everyone's willingness. All it takes is one person to be bold enough to speak up and others become courageous enough to speak up.

Willingness interrupts complacency, confuses silence, challenges protocol, and positions you for opportunity. We all have things we know we should be doing or changing, but we find ourselves avoiding conversations or compartmentalizing our feelings to avoid being uncomfortable. When we live in discomfort we often find ourselves channeling that energy into negativity whether it be living with a chip on our shoulder or harboring negativity that eats away at us. Reflect on a few past issues and the discomfort they caused you. Your willingness either added to you in addressing the issues or your lack of willingness cost you a piece of you. The piece that we lose is the piece that pushes us to do the work that repositions us.

A willing person is not satisfied with pointing issues out; they point issues out with the intent to resolve/remove the issue. Once an issue is pointed out, the energy we don't give it and the energy we give it not in the interest of resolution provides the issue opportunity to spread and become more complex. The answer is not to conform or ignore. The answer is addressing and adapting/adjusting; shifting our focus to creating/building our new normal.

A new normal pushes us away from settling by highlighting the discomfort we allowed to rule our lives. Discomfort, in this case, is not showing up, not stepping up, not giving your best effort and seamlessly moving forward, even though not giving your best hurts you. The same discomfort pushes us to focus on the external result versus the internal source because resolving what we feel we have to deal with, because it's visible, enables to continue to ignore what's not visible whether it's fear, self-esteem, or habits from thinking/living the only way we know.

Being willing to address the internal source trains us to be comfortable with getting uncomfortable. The anxiety we feel when we have to have a tough conversation/interaction or feeling overwhelmed in the face of the unknown begins to dwindle away as the discomfort no longer reigns over our being. The more work we do to address areas we question or where we have simply accepted less, we begin to witness a shift from being passive and reactive to being disruptive and proactive.

Through holding yourself to a higher level of accountability, your actions create a culture of willingness where life moves you (your business, your team, your family, etc.) from opportunity to opportunity versus us managing being stuck in mediocrity. Mediocrity is not a result it is state of being where you function in the misery you're unwilling to address. It's not okay to be okay with not asking why. Don't allow yourself to function in the misery of mediocrity, be willing to challenge yourself to get uncomfortable and do the work others won't.

Consistency

When being intentional about your days, consistency forces you to deal in truth. As you face instances where it's evident you (your perspective, your fear, your learned behaviors, etc.) are what's holding you back you have to choose to respond to the challenge of overcoming yourself or accepting the fact that you aren't willing to do the work to change your life. Consistency disciplines us by teaching us to ask more of ourselves without any excuses until giving more is our norm. Consistency trains us to think and behave differently. The discipline derived from consistency requires that we identify and address the external and internal factors that prevent us from believing in ourselves, stepping into opportunity, and giving our best in opportunity. So as we move forward with life we learn to expect them and defy them each time we sense them. The more we go against what we allowed to shape our mental and behavioral norms the more we feel uncomfortable with the associated energy because it does not agree with who we are. This is separation from who we used to be, where consistency stretches, pushes, challenges, and pulls you until you own the identity established through the discipline you've embodied.

As your being is redefined you come to realize your consistency has made you more in tune with your foundation or core values. This is critical, because it's evidence that how you see you has changed based on your thoughts, speech, and action…your being is now something you believe in, it's real not a far-fetched idea or concept. A newfound trust for yourself is important because the more you ask of yourself, the more obstacles you'll encounter.

Discipline doesn't mean life is now easy and free of challenges. Discipline means in learning to draw from your foundation your confidence doesn't waiver in the face of challenges. The trust your consistency has established pushes you past questioning yourself or your ability into operating from the truth you know versus the falsehoods you used to consider.

Emotions have the power to interrupt our discipline by creating distractions that lead to inconsistency. This is why emotional discipline is essential to being consistent; so we don't allow circumstances to evoke emotional reactions as opposed to disciplined responses. Our responses are based on perception and we are in charge of our perception. The only way to alter your perception is to be consistent in your effort to operate based on your belief system and not allow someone else's actions, thoughts, or beliefs to alter your being. Not only does this cause inconsistency in your being, but also hinders your ability to trust yourself.

The wrong perception teaches to give control to our circumstances, enabling emotions to drive inconsistent undisciplined behavior. The perception that consistency creates teaches us to stop accepting things as they are. It equips us with the confidence and determination to not only stop being passive about how we live our lives, but also be intentional about holding ourselves accountable to consistently ask more of ourselves to create the lives we desire.

Courage

Courage is essential because each of us face some form of opposition daily, and it takes courage to move forward despite the opposition we face. That being said, opposition should not and cannot impact you trying. Despite all the obstacles we've faced, are facing, or will face we must choose to walk in victory, not in question or defeat. You have figurative and literal scars that represent your past; they are not reminders of who you are, they are reminders that you had what it took to make it through. Live as the person courageous enough to fight and win, not as the person in the struggle, too fearful to fight back.

For years I dreamed about what life would be like after I left Luling. I thought about all the details from my house, to the car, traveling, my family, giving back, and my job. Years later when I was out of Luling, living my dream, and my life did not match that vision, I analyzed all the superficial reasons my life/career was stagnant, coming up with no answers. Then a friend recommended I read *The 50th Law* by Curtis "50 Cent" Jackson and Robert Greene.

The book focused on the various ways we allow fear, whether it is reasonable or not, to dictate our lives. It shared how 50 Cent applied instances where he overcame, inflicted, or capitalized on fear in his street life to instances in the entertainment business. What I grasped from this reading and my own experiences was the source of my fear was how I saw myself in my circumstances. The intimidation of the unfamiliar territory prevented me from facing my obstacles and embracing the challenge to learn how to believe in myself outside of my comfort zone.

How do you see yourself in your circumstances? Do you believe in what you have to add or does what you see as disadvantages like having a different upbringing or less school education make you feel inadequate? That is how I felt, inadequate or incapable, for most of my life. I avoided all situations where I felt I was risking embarrassing myself.

What I truly needed was to courageously believe the truth that the young man facing the fight had experiences, insight, and the significance in these overwhelming, unfamiliar settings to be successful. The same way not stepping up in college left me unsettled was the same way I felt whenever I went into a shell at the workplace. Courage is not introduced until we face opposition. So, like 50 Cent, I learned to embrace who my experiences helped create. Now, every day, I choose to face my fears, because the pain of regret hurts too much to continue to let fear and the lies I once accepted as my truth to ruin my life.

Accountability

It is very easy to be misguided in what we deem our responsibility, as our perspective impacts how we designate or determine value. Perspective triggers us to refuse responsibility in many instances out of selfishness or a poor vision of self. When we embrace purpose, we assume the responsibility of all that has been entrusted to us. In doing so, we have to trust that we have been equipped to fulfill the assignment purpose implies.

Ignoring responsibility has become normal in our world that teaches selfishness over selflessness. Talent, wisdom, a caring heart, a smile that lights up the room, intelligence, beauty, siblings, parents, relatives, less fortunate peers, workplace influence, online presence, stardom, children's innocence, a magnetic personality, humor—the list of all that has been entrusted to us goes on and on. But the influence of our culture devalues how we see these characteristics and diminishes our role as gatekeepers, leading us to neglect them, misuse them, and discredit them. Instead of selflessly cultivating what we are entrusted to empower others to do the same, we selfishly ignore others and abuse our gifts to serve our close-minded interests.

Understanding the magnitude of your choices and actions begins with knowing who you are and the value of what you possess. Stop allowing others and yourself to pigeon hole you, regarding your influence and ability. Your actions with the right intent have the potential to change the world. Instead of submitting to our responsibility we relinquish ownership to fit in supplementing the value we don't see with attention. I mentioned living this life as a teenager on into college when I was reluctant to be accountable as a leader. Now I witness the same behavior in adults on social media as they celebrate and boast about seeing their influence spread and inspire negativity across groups of people, but when faced with the challenge to be bold enough to do the same for positive impact, they can't be found. As meaningless as this behavior may seem, it is the infectious influence of being irresponsible that directly and indirectly encourages others to lead lives of running instead of accepting the responsibility of breaking cycles and destroying stereotypes.

Sometimes it takes seeing the negative influence you have had to understand you possess the power to make an impact. Your origins and your journey are the specific building blocks God uses to add significance to your being. That significance validates that you are special and validates the same for others He has designated for your message to reach. You are so much more valuable than you believe and give yourself credit for. If not for anything else I hope you choose to be accountable to validate this sentiment in someone else's life inspiring them to do the same for someone in their life.

Focus

In our overall focus or vision, we see greatness, but the intimidation of greatness is overwhelming when you don't embrace the day-to-day focus required to prevent you from getting in the way of doing the work to bring the vision to fruition. An overall focus brings light to our lives enlightens us and that guides us. The day-to-day focus that we embrace in how we operate is the submission to our vision that empowers us and becomes a beacon of light in the lives of others.

The journey doesn't come with the instant gratification that we see and experience through numerous facets so often today, so it's very important that you know the significance of your focus for your life, your family, your business, and your community, because a single moment can bring you closer to your vision or disrupt that portion of the journey. There will rarely be pats on the back or celebrations for reaching milestones which is the polar opposite of what we like to envision. In most cases true achievement and/or progression is overlooked because we honor the wrong things. The key is focusing on the reward of the journey so we honor becoming and celebrate ourselves versus seeking to be celebrated or celebrating what we gained or achieved based on other's perspective.

Stars arise daily in schools, law offices, corporations, churches, entertainment, and sports, as working toward the vision with the right intent separates them from the pack inciting others to push them to the forefront. It is ironic that being selfless separates us and encourages others to push us, but this is a reflection of the lack of empathy and surplus of selfishness in today's culture. The source of our intent as vessels makes us inclusive, but self-serving intent is exclusive. When our intent is misguided, we lose sight of His vision; without vision, we lose direction, bringing us to stagnancy that our selfishness pushes us to ignore or blinds us to. Ultimately, the stagnancy that we fail to address kills individuals, teams, businesses, churches, etc. from the inside out because leaders are so focused on their own interests they ignore the needs of those they serve.

Self-awareness enables us to identify how easy it is to engage in distractions as we work toward a goal. When we have trouble seeing ourselves as capable of overcoming our challenges, we seek out distractions because we would rather settle than face our internal struggles. We seek alternatives that comfort and/or numb us, including sex, drugs, alcohol, food, validation, enablers, and even arguments with naysayers. The irony of turning our focus to naysayers is that most naysayers see in us what we cannot see in ourselves. The noise of the world only catches our attention because it matches the noise we're already making internally. In accepting that the only opposition stopping us is us and committing to the focus needed to overcome ourselves, we discover the tools we possess to not only achieve but surpass our goals.

Patience

Adopting patience will always be a struggle when it is based on your ability to control your situation. It is a common assumption that patience means to be able to wait peacefully, but patience is more than waiting. One definition of patience is to be in delay. The struggle of patience is not the delay; the struggle is in our misinterpretation of our responsibility during the delay. As we close in on starting points, milestones, or deadlines, we experience anxiousness because of delays. Instead of making the delay beneficial to us by controlling what we can, we seek to control our circumstances. Once delay is determined, we must understand whether it is in school, work, sports, relationships, etc., patience is not simply stopping without complaining. Patience is utilizing delay to be at our best, not seeking to control our situation to best benefit you.

We can't control the timing or number of our opportunities, but we have full control of our execution in our opportunities. Living in expectation, means exhausting all resources and maximizing your efforts in preparation to capitalize when an opportunity is presented. Focusing on the delay causes you to lose control of the opportunity to be prepared because your energy goes to manipulation instead of investing.

If we fail to invest while delayed, we miss countless opportunities because preparation changes how we perceive obstacles and how we perceive ourselves regarding overcoming obstacles. Your breakthrough happens in your investment long before your moment. You seize your moment because you were patient enough to work while you waited which renewed your perspective to honor opportunity and built your confidence up enough to seize it. So don't wait...work. It's the information, insight, strength, endurance, experience that you gain in delay that changes how you view the path waiting to be created by you. As we receive revelation others are introduced to the power of patience through embracing delay versus self-destructing by trying to control what they can't.

Keep Your HeadDownPushing

What is your life saying? How is the way you are living impacting/influencing others? Are you in your own way or are you in control of your thoughts, speech, and action? Your life is already speaking, and you may or may not like what you are saying, but your opinion is irrelevant if you are not willing to take ownership of your circumstances and be the message you hope others will receive.

Football provided a tremendous platform where I encountered the power of several principles covered in this book, but my football experiences would've been meaningless without me deciding to get out of my own way.

The confusion in trying to accomplish something great came for me in the misguided pursuit of status and material things. I had to learn that our possessions, accomplishments, or status don't make us who we are, but who we are brings the possessions, accomplishments, and status to us. Life is not about working to get things; life is about working to become who He has called us to be so when those outside things come to us, they don't overshadow God or the investment that positioned us to attract those outside things to us. To have our HeadDownPushing is not only about the work we do to influence others, it is also doing and honoring the work on ourselves that has undone (and continues to undo) what we embraced that led us down the wrong path.

In the past, I allowed social standards to dictate how I saw myself and how I saw the world. Even though it hurt when I didn't speak up or when I failed to hold myself to a specific standard I still decided to forfeit the power my instincts suggested I had to seek outside approval for self-validation. How often do you follow your instincts in life? Are you as bold about your dreams as you are with your opinions on social media? Those dreams will remain exactly that as long as you are in your way. But if you choose to see you like He sees you, you can begin living those dreams immediately.

Even though I've always wanted to influence others to be their best I never truly understood the impact we can have on someone by simply being. My mentality has always been to work with the intent of changing culture, but in regards of stepping into my rightful place a bold leader I was fearful of the response and the responsibility. Allowing that fear to determine my actions caused a lot of disappointment throughout the years of my life. Then one day I realized I was fed up with living in fear and the endless cycle of excuses and aimlessness that were holding me captive in mediocrity. From that day on I've strived to not allow a greater influence on my life than Jesus Christ and my desire to not have any regrets.

Since, I made it a point to focus on the work before me and do what came natural to me as a leader in leading by example. Through doing I was thrust into leadership role after leadership role. I'd already embraced the responsibility and my actions suggested I prioritized doing the right thing over how others felt about it. Even though I saw big the picture, I was in an internal battle because I saw the power of actions and character, but at the same time I was taught notoriety was what I should be chasing by the world around me. Then, through witnessing transformation in others, God revealed the power of our being through simply doing and it changed my life. I was humbled in that moment as I understood the value He sees in all individuals. I not only understood how I never needed to seek validation again and to live like it, but also I understood it was my responsibility to teach anyone who would listen the same.

For me to embrace that power, I had to understand who I am in Christ and the only way I could learn who I truly am was through a relationship. A big problem we have with revelation is that we like to run back into life and leave God behind only to end up searching for Him all over again. This is where relationship becomes important because in relationship, not only do we not want to go forward without Him, but we also don't make plans without Him; because we only want to be where He wants us to be.

As my relationship has grown, my perception of myself changed. As my perception of myself has evolved, my expectations of myself has evolved as well. I could not be faithful and be at peace being the person I used to be or thinking like I did before. The faith that supports relationship activates a humility that forces you to revisit and remove you from being in God's way. As you revisit every situation, scenario, or encounter you experienced, you strip away that selfish, prideful perspective and relive it through your newly embraced humble perspective and see God's intent in you and through you.

As we see more of God's intent, renewed perspective encourages us to push forward. As we push forward, we begin to experience the principles, the more we exhibit them, the more they show up and reinforce each other. Embodying the principles in our daily journey enables us to exceed our own expectations and encourages others to do the same. Your faith invokes a willingness to step out of your comfort zone and the courage to not turn away from opportunity. The experiences increase your focus, which garners a patient consistency due to a humble perspective that pushes you to be accountable to all that has been entrusted to you. These principles intertwine as they flow in and out of our being, bringing us face to face with what we have been (past message), who we are (our current message), and who we are becoming (God's message).

We all have so many things we want to do or dream of doing, but we allow fear or lies to prevent us from living the life we desire. The only way things will change in your life is acting on your desires. Your life is demanding that you step onto the playing field and stop being a spectator. You are of too great a value to not impact the world around you by simply bringing your most authentic you to life and putting forth the effort into being your best daily.

Every one of us at one time or another has found ourselves stuck in time while everything around us has moved forward. Those who acknowledge, adjust, and push forward are the leaders of our culture. Instead of focusing on what they don't like, they are focused on how they will continue to flourish despite unfavorable circumstances. This ability is not limited to one or a few people. We all have this ability, but being successful going forward starts with redefining who you are and what you have to contribute then applying it in your own way.

Embracing these principles doesn't make life easy or guarantee success. The principles are tools to help you get out of your own way and encourage others around you to do the same. These principles don't require you to have a relationship as I stated before, but relationship is the lifeline of the faith that teaches you to embrace the value of the journey as it coaches you, consoles you, sustains you, picks you up, guards you, redirects you, holds you accountable, and pushes you back into the game when you fall off track, which is inevitable.

They say great things come from pain. Without allowing ourselves to fully experience the pain then choosing to grow through it, instead being imprisoned by our pain, we can't experience our greatness on the other side. This book touches on a portion of the pain I experienced that made me exhausted with the life I was leading. If you are exhausted, unsatisfied, or miserable in your circumstances, you have to do something about it. In changing your life I hope this book helps you identify that you are further along than you gave yourself credit for and you not only have the ability to create the environment you live in, but God is waiting for you to do so.

In realizing my life is a message, I also realized I have to navigate the unchartered waters of living intentionally. With every aspiration there is opposition that attempts to make you forget who you are in order to drive you back to your comfort zone where you can live safely in mediocrity. I thrived in my comfort zone, on the sidelines of life for years, not even realizing the game was in play. I was awesome at being busy doing nothing. As a matter of fact we all are when we're determined to not be something. After finding myself in this space again and again whether it was during High School, in College, in the streets, or in the workplace I realized the sidelines are noisy and overcrowded with people who are content with talking, complaining, sulking, being afraid, being angry, and refusing accountability. The noise of the sidelines reminds me of the pain of being stuck, and that I have to be intentional or my lack thereof will cost me. The crowd reminds me of how slippery the slope of negativity is and how hard it is to leave a place you've settled in.

I've been in the Healthcare industry for 11 years now and all that has been required of me has not ceased to change. The more I seek, the more I first have to give. Things are the same for Public Speaking as well. The more I give, the more doors open requiring that I ask more of myself. Whether it's the opportunity to speak at different Schools, Sports Teams, Non-profits, Businesses, & Churches I continue to seek more growth for more impact. Also, the more I invest in growth the more confidence I have to make myself available which creates more opportunity. For instance, I was recently ordained as Associate Pastor on September 23rd, 2018 of New Beginnings International House of Blessings in Luling TX. It wasn't something I was seeking, but something in my service that moved the church enough to bless me with the assignment.

Some people would focus on the obligation of the role, but the only obligation I can see or feel is my obligation to God. I know that if I strive to please Him everything else will take care of itself. This role is not for me to teach, this role is for me to learn. So I thank God ahead of time for the pain of progression while he takes me to a new level of leadership as I learn to submit even more.

Each of us has a new battle yearly, monthly, weekly, daily, and sometimes hourly. In writing this book I've realized I'm already a winner so I don't have to fool me, I just need to believe in me. So what battle are you avoiding? Stop running and let go! Get out of your own way and submit to the assignment life has brought before you because you did not make it to this place as you are by chance. The moment you decide to go directly at your fears without holding anything back is the moment you begin to win. When you see you as the winner you are, life changes because you are no longer held captive by fear, limitations, and acceptance. You are free not only to dream, but also emboldened and informed enough to understand the importance of being intentional about submitting yourself to living the dream daily. When you accept purpose it's humbling, invigorating, and exciting as you find yourself living your dreams, but what makes the fight against yourself worth having is knowing because you submitted someone else will win the battle against themselves. Those wins…His wins…That is why I keep my Head…Down…Pushing.

ACKNOWLEDGEMENTS

I wanted to take the time to thank a few special people for simply being themselves and breathing into me what led me to write this book. If I missed anyone charge it to my mind and not my heart. Thank you to my parents, Billy and Rhonda Roberts, for being my everything. I am because of you. There is nothing that I've done or that I do that did not begin with your influence so I thank you because your sacrifice and selflessness gave me insight, intrigue, love, and integrity that many aren't blessed to receive. Your commitment will forever keep me accountable. I thank you for your lives because I know that's what you both gave to Pooh and I. To my wife Monica, you are an extension of God on earth. He blessed me with a wife that I'm so grateful for that the only way I feel like I can honor you is to honor Him. Thanks for your commitment to Him to grow with me, to inspire me, to support me, to push me, to add to me, and to allow me as we make the most of this thing called life. Jackson, my first born, thank you for being the special boy you are. You changed my life from the day I learned of your conception and your being continues to mold me daily because your free spirit and pureness of heart challenge me to get in position to be everything I can to serve you. Emory, my Princess, thank you for needing me and not being too scared or prideful to let me know it. Your transparency and vulnerability inform me of my responsibility to be here for you, to let you do you, to learn from you, to show you how a man should conduct himself and how a man should treat you. Your strong will chastises me as I bear the task of protecting that, but it's a blessing in and out of each day as I learn to do so. Jaylon, my bonus son, thank you for continuously reintroducing me to humility. Being the oldest child means you have it the roughest as we learn how to

Acknowledgements

parent. As a step-parent I had no clue what I was signing up for, but what I've learned is to always ask, "what can I do better". Your light is bright and it's my job to make sure you know it and own it...not based on the approval of others or what you possess, but solely based on God's fulfilling of His promise to you. To my In-Laws, Charles and Sandra Beridon, thank you for loving me like your own and thank you for everything you do. Ya'll are the definition of family. I know the life we live would be impossible without you all so thank you for your support, love, time, and presence because it truly makes a difference to our family. To Paw-Paw, Eddie McKinney, your wisdom is endless. Thank you for you unfiltered truth, pouring into my spirit, and for being the foundation for our family. To Mee-Maw, Patricia McKinney, thank you for the love you gave me. You had a way of loving every grandchild in your own way that made us all feel special and that will forever live on in each of us. Uncle Terry thank you for passing down that "it". I never have felt like your nephew because you treated me like your son. You always made me feel special so I learned to embrace that because of how I saw you...different/special. Little did I know you were teaching me to be like you in so many ways, so just know "Doc" gonna stay strong through faith and won't quit just like you Unc. Aunt Bev you are the most humble and selfless person I know. I don't think any of us worry too hard because we know we got you. Thank you for being the family's glue. Your life showed me Auntie, it planted seeds of greatness and continues to do so. You made "it" tangible and there is no value that can be placed on that. Thank you for loving old Chandler (me) differently because it made and makes a difference. Aunt Cheryl and Aunt Yvette, ya'll are the true definition of Aunties. Thank ya'll for simply being ya'll. What ya'll do means something and makes a difference in all of our lives. The unconditional love ya'll give this family, the example ya'll set as women and mothers, as professionals, as servants, your loyalty, your selflessness, and your resiliency is second to none. We love ya'll and all of our uncles. Aunt Catherine, thank you and Aunt Pearlene for stepping up. We are forever indebted to ya'll. I

Acknowledgements

wouldn't have a grandmother on my father's side if it weren't for you, but because of you I can't claim to feel that void. To my only little (First) cousin on my dad's side, Lee Fields, I love you with all my heart. Thank you for continuing to fight for your life. Go live your dreams and never stop making sure your mom is good. To my Aunt, Diane Fields, thank you for simply loving me. You're such a beautiful person and to feel loved by such a pure spirit is a feeling that can't be put into words. To Bernadette Spears, my Other Mother, thank you for your prayers, love, support, consistency, and for simply being you. You have always challenged me and never allowed me settle regardless of how comfortable I may be. Sometimes kids need to hear something from someone other than Mom or Dad and you never failed in that department. I'm truly grateful for your obedience and caring spirit that always checks in at the right time. To Robert Fields, thank you for pouring that word into us at a young age. Even though it wasn't fun, the experience was impactful. To Ian Buchanan, this is a product of our prayer time. Thank you for sharing your journey with me which continues to motivate me and thanks for keeping me accountable through pushing and questioning me. Thank you for taking the time to help me with editing as well because that helped get me to the finish line. To Kerry Lampkin, thanks for always encouraging me, believing in me, and sharing your journey with me because your walk speaks loudly and definitely challenged me to keep faithfully moving forward. Keep being the special light that you are…this is only still the beginning. To Ameera York, thanks for cheering me on, reminding me of who I am, and never allowing me to settle. You relit my fire by challenging me to step into my rightful role as a leader. That can never be repaid, but because of you I will never let that fire be put out again. To Kingsley, Aspen, and Joshua Ross thank you for allowing me to serve with ya'll. Your work ethic and willingness to pursue your dreams is infectious. Our connection and the energy I receive in my spirit from ya'll is something I hold near and dear to my heart. To Paula Houston, thanks for the love and your consistency. You have never asked for anything, you simply

Acknowledgements

just gave me the most valuable gift you could…your time and yourself. For that I am forever grateful. Hope to keep making you proud. To Baylor Barbee, thanks for pushing me, enlightening me, sharing with me, working for me, working with me, encouraging, me, believing in me, and seeing in me what I can't sometimes see in myself. Thanks brother because your life influences me to go get everything I desire. Can't wait to see what you do next! To Trent Shelton, my lil bro that became my big bro in so many ways. Thank you for simply being you. I hate missing any opportunity I have to serve you because it truly is an honor. I'm proud of you man and your continued progression. You've always been set apart and it's a blessing to the world now that you have more understanding of God's doing so in your life. You pulled me into this arena, thanks for knowing when I didn't! To my Luling family…wow! Thank you for nurturing, loving, teaching, protecting, supporting, challenging, questioning, following, celebrating, and championing one of your sons. Thank you for smiling on me, expecting of me, and allowing me to be me. Thank you for loving our family and taking care of us during a tough time…Please know I cherish every reinforced moral, honorable value, and seed planted in my life. I'll never forget where I come from. To my Houston/Dallas family and friends (Including Monica's family, friends, and their parents) thank you for the love. It is deeply felt and appreciated. You don't have to be thoughtful, caring, loving, and selfless, but you are and for that I want you know I consider you all a true blessing. I am truly grateful for each and every one of you. Thank you, Mrs. Gene Chase, for the love and reassurance. Your warmth and care brought me comfort and peace. At a time when children are so delicate you became a presence outside of my family that gave me the willingness to just be and the confidence to know I would be alright in this world. Who and what you are is evident in your daughter, Rose Chase-Smith, as she is a tremendous individual. Her journey is an inspiration and something all of us from Luling to celebrate. Mrs. Paula Horne, thank you for giving me your all. Your loving spirit and commitment was felt daily. You made me not just want to go to school, but go and be

Acknowledgements

great. Phil Grandjean, thank you for taking care of me. Thank you for teaching me the significance of the little things and that I have to fight for my dreams in this thing we call life. I hate the time it seems like we missed, but I'll take it every time if it means losing the time we had. To Craig Deberry, thank you for allowing me to find my way as a leader. Most coaches let their ego get in their way, but you trusted and allowed me to be the guiding voice and you stepped in accordingly. This taught me to trust me at early age because I couldn't get the most out of everyone else if I didn't believe in myself...Thank you. To Harold "2-9" Jackson, thank you for believing in me. When you had no reason you gave me a chance. Thank you for your wisdom, your support, your encouragement, and for fighting for me. You completely changed my college football experience and where my life was headed. To David Hill, thanks for holding me accountable. You were the first person to teach me about my responsibility to something greater than me. I didn't like the talks, but I got it and it never left. To Pastor Robert Douglas and Dr. Karen Douglas thank you for loving on me, giving me an opportunity, taking me in, and for being the best versions of yourselves which still to this day provides us with something to aspire to. Your willingness, humility, and selflessness truly blessed my life. To Coach Cook, thanks for never laying off of me and holding me accountable, I needed that. I also needed to learn to express myself and not have it held against me. Thank for allowing me to be me while still challenging me to be better. To Buck and Joc, thank ya'll for being Coaches and Big Brothers that demanded of us. Ya'll taught us how to believe in the work we put in, to give of ourselves without looking for anything in return, and that it's cool to be about something. To my San Antonio bros. Thank ya'll for the love, for receiving me, treating me like one of ya'll, for pushing me by doing more with your lives, and for showing me what true friendship is. I missed ya'll! Jonathan Evans, you were a role model for us all at BU. You knew who you were and stood on that with no shame and that gave me courage to be me. When I didn't know what I had in you as a friend you remained loyal to me.

Acknowledgements

Thank you for being true to yourself, being a true friend, and thank you for challenging me as a man. Thank you Maurice Lane for being a true friend bro! Appreciate and love you more than you know. Tank, my brother from another mother. What's understood doesn't have to be said! Love you Man! To Antoine Murphy and Matthew Johnson (MJ), thank ya'll for loving me man and pouring into my spirit. It's felt and held near to my heart. I hope you both feel the love I have for you. Just know my effort to get it in everything I do is not in vain. Just know I'm pulling for you. Aaron Karas, thanks for always being a presence that does not have to be seen to be felt. You're awesome man and your journey is impactful to the people who love you brother. Keep going, because your life alone pushes us to be better. To Kevin Shandy, thank you for believing in me and presenting me with opportunity. I hope what I've given has been as valuable to you all as what I received is to me. To the Sugar Land Sugar Speakers Toastmaster's club thank you for taking me in and challenging me be what I set out to be. Thank you specifically to, Tim DeRosa and Keith Romaine. Your critique and constructive criticism challenged me to work harder and ask more of myself as a speaker. Because of your commitment to your role I grew at a rapid pace and to a place I only hoped I could reach. Because of that process I know I can take the next steps to take my career to the next level. To Theresa Strong, thank you for the countless opportunities. I literally have grown up through my experiences with Bel-Inizio. The time I've spent serving with you all has been invaluable and I thank you deeply because your team, family (love your mother and Bette), and the ladies you serve have been a blessing. To Regina Walker, thank you for having me and supporting me. Your warm spirit touches me every time we meet. You are truly a phenomenal person that makes the world a better place. To Wendy Jones, thank you for everything you've sown into my spirit. Some people give us tangible things, but others touch our souls. You are a very special individual, keep letting God have His way because "eyes have not seen, ears have not heard." To Mama Sheila Ann, thank you for pushing me and not allowing me to

Acknowledgements

produce anything less than my best. You brought me in, made me learn no matter what it took for me to get it, and because of you I'll never be the same in the workplace. You made me learn to believe in me in a setting that I didn't think I belonged in. On top of that, you treated me like your own which enabled me to be comfortable being me. I can never repay you for what you did for my life so just know I carry a piece of you wherever I go. To Brandy Rivera, Holly Hernandez, and Carmen Smith, thank you all for taking care of me and seeing something in me that I couldn't see myself at times. Just want you know that feeling like someone cared truly made a difference. Prefeance Baker, Tracy Baines, and Mrs. Versey, thank you, you all loved on me and encouraged me as your own. You fed me physically and spiritually. Every meal, every conversation, and your loving spirits touched me and breathed life into me. To Katrina Thompson, Chawana Smith, and Mary Hunter thanks for letting me be me. Thanks for being my safe haven, always looking out for me, taking care of me, and being a source of unconditional love. Ya'll are my grown-up home away from home. To Earl Jumawan, thanks for sharing with me, being an ear, for working with me, for looking out for me, and for your time. We spend a lot of time sharing, so I aim to execute so that my actions push you as your actions have definitely pushed me. Mike Bennett, man you definitely had your HeadDownPushing! You plucked me right up from a rough patch and never blinked. You just said go get it and made sure I was doing so. Thank you for being a phenomenal human being who made a difference in this world. I thank God you shared a piece of your greatness with a little country boy. You showed me the value of authenticity and the difference doing the little things makes. To Donna Poole and Derick Perkins, thanks for being great leaders. Your attention to detail and ability to be personable, but professional are like no other. Donna, you don't operate like others and I hope you never do because your significance is undeniable. Derick, as a black male it's refreshing to see you be true to you without compromise nor apology. Thanks for being someone that others like myself can look up to and take something from. Mike

Acknowledgements

Hill, thank you for taking a chance on me and taking care of me. You didn't have to, but you did. You're one of the best in the business and I can't say there are many built like you...stay that way. Lisa Schillaci, thank you for being a tremendous leader. I've never witnessed what I witnessed from you as a leader. You not only challenged us, but you equipped us. You didn't climb up to look down, you created a path and broke through to new territory. Then you sought to bring your team along versus leaving them behind. You saw something in me and treated me as such. Thanks for encouraging me and encouraging me to let my light shine. Beverly Gault, thank you for empowering me and trusting me. When everything suggested you should turn your back on me you came to me, made me aware, gave me your full support, encouraged me, and then allowed my work to speak for itself versus acting based on false reports. Thanks for mentoring me and getting more from me. To Amy Depedro, thank you for modeling what it takes then allowing me to find my way. You're a constant reminder that leaders need to know how to swim too. To Dr. Tony Evans thank you taking the time out our senior year and serving as our Team Chaplain. I mean you just don't people of stature do what you did. Your humility, servanthood, and wisdom is out of this world. I'm still learning from those Friday night Bible Studies and Saturday morning services. We had no clue of the value of what you were pouring into us, but I want you to know (As I already know you do looking at our lives) it was not in vain. One day you asked, "Is everything okay?" I replied yes sir and you knew it wasn't the truth, and you let me know you were there if I needed. That truly blessed me. Dr. Ralph Douglas-West (Pas), thank you for being a phenomenal teacher. When I moved to Houston I needed a church home and it was your teaching that captured me, steadied me, fed me, challenged me, pushed me, and invigorated me. It had to be God that led me to pull over to a random church on a Sunday morning as I longed to be fed. Thanks for your commitment to excellence. To Pastor Robert Simpson Jr. Thank you for welcoming my family, caring for us, and loving on us. Even beyond that, thank

Acknowledgements

you for being a true servant and teaching through action what true servanthood looks like as a Man, Husband, Father, Pastor and Mentor. Our journey is merely beginning and I'm grateful to have you to guide me. Dennis Brown, thank you for mentoring me on this journey of speaking and writing. Your insight and encouragement has been invaluable. Your humility, humor, and thoughtfulness are also noted because they are validation that you don't just talk, but you live the things you teach. To Alexis McClinton, thank you for never settling and never allowing me to settle. You constantly strive to take your life to new heights and the beautiful thing about it is you hold everyone around you accountable to do the same. To Maresah, thanks for going to get it and constantly challenging yourself. I love you and hope you get everything God has for you because you deserve it. To Matthew and Edwin, thank you for still looking up to me. I know I'm far from perfect, but you still truly love and honor your cousin. That's pressure, but it's good pressure because it keeps me accountable. Just know I honor both of you as well. The men that you've become is something to be proud of so know that I truly smile and poke my chest out your big cousin. To Chloe and Kasi thanks for fighting. You had every excuse to choose not to fight, but you still chose to win. Now it's time for us to take it to the next level and pay it back. To my Corpus family…thank you for always loving me even when time and location kept us apart. True love changes us and the love you all share with me makes me grateful because it has changed me. To my Luling (and other small town brethren) and Baylor brothers; me encouraging others started with ya'll. You not only allowed me to be your leader, but you challenged me in that role. When I stepped up, spoke up, or distanced myself from negativity you joined me, encouraged me, and saluted me. You trusted me and expected of me. When I didn't know, you taught me. When I didn't have you gave to me. When I was wrong you allowed me to make it right without holding it against me. When I second guessed you chastised me. When I didn't step up you held me accountable. More than anything though you responded in your own specific ways when I was lost,

Acknowledgements

overwhelmed, or simply in need. You took the reins to lead me, you supported me, you comforted me, you loved me, and you always treated me as what I could be. To all of you, thank you, and my only hope is that my life at one point or another has blessed you as much as your lives have blessed mine.

www.ingramcontent.com/pod-product-compliance
Lightning Source LLC
Chambersburg PA
CBHW070602100426
42744CB00006B/376